UNMASKED: THE ART OF RECOGNIZING FALSEHOODS

The Tools and Tactics of Truth-Detection

Deborah Galiffa Fliehman

D.G. Fliehman Publishing

ISBN Paperback: 979-8-9920439-2-1

ISBN Hardback: 979-8-9920439-3-8

Disclaimer

This book, *Unmasked: The Art of Recognizing Falsehoods,* includes information and examples sourced through ChatGPT, an AI language model designed to assist with general information and creative ideas. While ChatGPT is a valuable tool, it is not infallible and may inadvertently provide inaccurate or incomplete information. The author has made every effort to verify and contextualize the information presented; however, the author cannot be held responsible for any factual inaccuracies, omissions, or errors originating from the AI. Readers are encouraged to use their discretion and consult additional reliable sources when interpreting or applying the content in this book.

Dedication

This book is dedicated to:

Steve, Sara, Lauren, Matt, Reese, Cy

I hope to help create a future filled with honesty, dignity, equality, and respect for all.

i

Contents

Chapter One:
Purpose of This Book

L earning to communicate with integrity enhances every aspect of life. During an election year, exploring the realities of truth and falsehood is intriguing. Elections highlight the importance of honesty in public discourse. They bring campaign promises, advertisements, debates, and media commentary to the forefront. The stakes are exceptionally high, and the consequences of misinformation become pronounced. False claims or distorted facts can sway opinions and alter the future of an entire nation. Writing during this time allows exploration of how truth shapes decision-making in a democracy, playing a critical role in ensuring citizens make informed choices.

Media is critical in scrutinizing claims, countering misinformation, and ensuring transparency during an election. Different types of media approach this task in varied and complementary ways, each contributing uniquely to the identification of lies and misrepresentations:

1. Traditional News Outlets

- **Print Media:** Newspapers and magazines often provide in-depth investigative journalism, analyzing campaign claims, political ads, and speeches. Their long form reporting allows for nuanced critiques of complex issues.

- **Television:** News programs on channels like CNN, BBC, or local networks provide real-time coverage, fact-checking segments, and debates. They bring immediate analysis of political events to a broad audience.

- **Radio:** Public and talk radio channels engage in political discourse, hosting discussions and interviews with experts who analyze the validity of claims.

2. Fact-Checking Organizations

- Independent platforms like PolitiFact, FactCheck.org, or Snopes specialize in verifying statements made by politicians, advertisements, and media outlets. They use rigorous methodologies to categorize claims as true, false, or somewhere in between.

- Other media often cite their findings to hold political figures accountable.

3. Social Media Platforms

- Platforms like Twitter, Facebook, and Instagram amplify political messages and are also breeding grounds for misinformation. However, they provide users with tools to report false information.

- Social media companies partner with fact-checkers and employ algorithms to label false or misleading content.

- Viral campaigns by advocacy groups or individuals often aim to educate voters by debunking myths circulating online.

4. Alternative and Independent Media

- Smaller, independent outlets often focus on specific issues or marginalized perspectives. While some are known for investigative rigor, others may perpetuate misinformation, necessitating careful consumption.

- Podcasts and blogs provide alternative perspectives, fostering a more participatory form of media engagement. However, they vary in reliability.

5. Citizen Journalism

- With the advent of smartphones, ordinary citizens now document events in real time, exposing inconsistencies or corroborating claims. Citizen journalists often operate on social media and can bring immediacy and authenticity to public scrutiny. Without editorial oversight, the accuracy of these types of reports varies widely.

6. Academic and Research Institutions

- Universities and think tanks conduct studies to assess the accuracy of political messaging, providing scholarly perspectives that delve deeper into issues like voter influence and media manipulation. Their data and reports are authoritative resources for media professionals and the public.

7. Entertainment Media

- Satirical shows like The Daily Show or Last Week Tonight use humor to highlight falsehoods and inconsistencies in political rhetoric. Though not traditional journalism, they can raise public awareness and encourage critical thinking.

Collaboration and Challenges

Cross-platform collaborations often emerge during election cycles, uniting traditional and digital media with fact-checkers to provide comprehensive analyses.

Challenges include the speed with which information is spread on social media and echo chambers (an environment or ecosystem in which participants encounter information that amplifies or reinforces their preexisting beliefs by communication and repetition inside a closed system and insulated from rebuttal. (Wikipedia)) and the difficulty of reaching individuals already convinced by misinformation.

The media's diversity ensures that misinformation can be tackled from multiple angles through analysis, real-time reporting, expert opinions, and public participation. Citizens' engagement with various media types is critical to discerning truth and making informed choices in a democracy.

Policymakers play a critical role in addressing the spread of misinformation during election cycles through various actions and strategies:

Legislation - developing and enacting laws that promote transparency in political advertising, requiring accountability from social media platforms, and imposing penalties for disseminating false information can help mitigate the impact of misinformation.

Collaboration with Tech Companies - policymakers can work with social media and technology companies to create guidelines and practices that reduce the spread of false information, such as implementing stricter content moderation policies and enhancing fact-checking partnerships.

Public Awareness Campaigns - initiating campaigns to educate the public about misinformation and its effects can empower voters to critically evaluate information and encourage responsible sharing practices.

Funding Research and Resources - supporting research on the effects of misinformation and funding initiatives aimed at improving media literacy can help communities better understand and combat misinformation during elections.

Establishing Independent Oversight - creating independent bodies to monitor and report on misinformation trends, particularly during election periods, can provide essential data and insights to policymakers and the public.

Fostering Collaboration Across Sectors - encouraging partnerships between government agencies, civil society organizations, academic institutions, and media outlets can promote a coordinated approach to tackling misinformation.

Ensuring Electoral Integrity - implementing measures to secure electoral processes, such as auditing election technologies and safeguarding against foreign interference, can help build public trust and reduce the susceptibility to misinformation.

Providing Clear Guidelines for Political Speech - establishing clear standards for political discourse can help set expectations for honesty and accountability, making it easier to identify and combat misinformation.

By taking these actions, policymakers can play a vital role in creating an environment where voters are better protected from misinformation, ultimately fostering healthier democratic processes during election cycles.

Citizens can be better educated about distinguishing between reliable and unreliable sources of information through several approaches:

Media Literacy Education - incorporating media literacy programs in schools and community centers can teach individuals how to critically analyze information sources, recognize bias, and evaluate the credibility of content.

Workshops and Training Sessions - hosting workshops led by experts in journalism, fact-checking, or digital literacy can provide practical tools and techniques for assessing information quality.

Access to Online Resources - creating and disseminating resources, such as guides or checklists for evaluating sources, can help individuals understand what to look for when encountering information online.

Promotion of Fact-Checking Tools - encouraging the use of fact-checking websites and tools as part of daily information consumption can empower citizens to verify claims before sharing or believing them.

Encouragement of Critical Thinking - facilitating discussions and activities that promote critical thinking skills can help individuals question the validity of information and the motivations behind it.

Public Awareness Campaigns - initiating campaigns that raise awareness about the dangers of misinformation and the importance of verifying facts can inspire citizens to take a more proactive approach to their media consumption.

Collaboration with Libraries - partnering with public libraries to offer resources and training focused on information literacy can provide a trustworthy environment for citizens to learn.

Engagement with Diverse Perspectives - encouraging individuals to seek information from a variety of sources can help them develop a more nuanced understanding of issues and recognize how different narratives can shape perceptions.

By implementing these strategies, citizens can enhance their ability to discern reliable sources from unreliable ones, leading to more informed decision-making and greater resilience against misinformation.

Individuals can employ several strategies to verify the credibility of information encountered on social media:

Check the Source - look for information from reputable news organizations, established fact-checking sites, or expert sources. Verify the author's credentials and background.

Cross-Reference Information - compare the information with other reliable sources. If multiple credible outlets report the same story, it is more likely to be accurate.

Examine the Evidence - look for supporting evidence such as statistics, research references, or firsthand accounts. Credible information typically includes sources that can be verified independently.

Analyze the Content - be cautious of sensationalized headlines or emotionally charged language, which can indicate bias or misinformation. Assess whether the content is balanced and fair.

Check the Date - ensure the information is current and relevant. Sometimes, outdated information can resurface and mislead individuals about an ongoing situation.

Seek Expert Opinions - for complex topics, consider consulting experts or academic resources that specialize in the subject matter for more accurate insights.

Use Fact-Checking Tools - utilize platforms like Snopes, FactCheck.org, or PolitiFact to verify claims and check for any fact-checking reports related to the information.

Be Mindful of Bias - consider the potential biases of the source and your own biases. Awareness of these factors can help you evaluate information more objectively.

By using these strategies, individuals can enhance their ability to discern credible information and make informed decisions based on accurate facts. It's important that the citizens expect politicians to assume ethical responsibilities, and for the media, and the public to engage honestly.

Media professionals hold a significant power to shape public perception, and their role in maintaining accuracy is of utmost importance. In a world where the line between truth and falsehood is often blurred, the need for fact- checking, scrutiny, and truth promotion is crucial. Addressing these themes is an opportunity to inform and a call to action. In a society inundated with information, it is necessary to empower people to assess what they encounter critically.

This mission fosters independence and empowers us to question and sift through information mindfully. Everyone has a responsibility to help combat misinformation and to influence others to develop critical thinking skills. Combating misinformation and fostering critical thinking are essential for maintaining a healthy, informed, democratic society.

Here's why this responsibility is vital:

Upholding Democracy - Misinformation erodes the foundation of democracy by misleading voters and skewing their understanding of issues, candidates, or policies. Critical thinking helps individuals assess claims and make decisions based on facts rather than manipulation.

When falsehoods dominate public discourse, they undermine trust in democratic institutions, elections, and governance. Combating misinformation safeguards the legitimacy of democratic systems.

Preventing Polarization and Conflict - Misinformation often exploits existing social, political, or cultural divides, deepening polarization, and sowing discord. Encouraging critical thinking promotes dialogue and mutual understanding. False narratives can incite violence, discrimination, or harmful policy decisions. A population equipped to discern truth can prevent such outcomes.

Protecting Public Health and Safety - In contexts like health crises, misinformation about vaccines, treatments, or public health guidelines can lead to unnecessary illness or death. Critical thinking empowers people to evaluate scientific evidence and prioritize safety. Misinformation often thrives on fear. By promoting critical thinking, individuals can challenge fear- based narratives and make rational decisions.

Strengthening the Social Fabric - A culture that values truth fosters trust between individuals, communities, and institutions. Misinformation erodes trust and leads to cynicism. Shared understanding and factual agreement allow collective problem-solving, which is vital for addressing societal challenges like climate change or economic inequality.

Empowering Individuals - Misinformation often exploits cognitive biases, emotions, or a lack of knowledge. Critical thinking equips individuals with the tools to question sources, identify biases, and resist manipulation. Combating misinformation encourages intellectual curiosity, pushing individuals to seek diverse perspectives and continuously learn.

Ethical Responsibility - Spreading misinformation, whether intentional or not, can have real-world consequences. Everyone has a moral duty to contribute positively to public discourse. A society that values truth holds individuals, media, and institutions accountable for the information they share.

Ensuring Resilience Against Emerging Threats - The rise of AI, deepfakes, (a realistic-looking image, video, or audio recording that has been manipulated using artificial intelligence (AI)), and sophisticated propaganda tools make misinformation harder to detect. A population with critical thinking skills is better equipped to adapt and respond to these challenges. Authoritarian regimes often use misinformation to suppress dissent and control narratives. Critical thinking helps protect freedoms by empowering citizens to question authority and demand transparency.

Individuals can contribute in several ways:

1. **Verify Before Sharing**: Fact-check information, especially on social media.

2. **Teach and Encourage Critical Thinking**: Foster skills like skepticism, logical reasoning, and source evaluation in others, especially younger generations.

3. **Engage in Respectful Dialogue**: Challenge misinformation without resorting to hostility, encouraging productive discussions.

4. **Support Reliable Media:** Amplify and subscribe to reputable journalism to counterbalance the spread of falsehoods.

5. **Lead by Example**: Model responsible behavior by avoiding sensationalism and prioritizing truth over convenience.

By taking collective responsibility, individuals protect themselves and contribute to a society where truth, accountability, and reason prevail - ensuring a brighter and more equitable future for all.

We can play a part in shaping a more truthful society. Misinformation, particularly rampant on social media and in news outlets, needs to be confronted. By raising awareness and offering insights into recognizing false information, I aim to energize others to be more discerning and proactive in their approach to information.

Confronting misinformation, especially on social media and in news outlets, is critical because it impacts individual beliefs, societal stability, and democratic processes. Societies function on shared truths, whether in science, history, or governance, and misinformation distorts these truths, creating confusion and undermining trust in facts. When falsehoods spread unchecked, they damage the credibility of institutions, media, and individuals, leading to widespread skepticism and disengagement.

A democracy relies on an informed electorate, but misinformation skews public understanding of candidates, policies, and events, potentially altering election outcomes. Furthermore, false narratives can be weaponized to manipulate public opinion, suppress votes, or delegitimize electoral processes, threatening democratic institutions.

The harm caused by misinformation extends beyond politics. In public health, for example, false information about vaccines or medical treatments can encourage risky behaviors, reject proven science, and lead to widespread harm.

Misinformation can also incite violence, fuel hate crimes, and cause panic, destabilizing communities, and threatening lives. On a social level, misinformation exacerbates polarization, as social media algorithms often prioritize sensational or emotionally charged content that reinforces political and social divisions.

This creates echo chambers where people are less likely to encounter differing perspectives, deepening misunderstanding, and discouraging productive dialogue. Vulnerable populations are particularly affected, as misinformation exploits harmful stereotypes, spreads scams, and marginalizes underrepresented voices.

Economic and environmental stability are also at risk. False financial information can lead to scams that harm individual livelihoods and economic stability, while misinformation about ecological issues, like climate change, delays critical action on global challenges.

Social media amplifies these threats by instantly enabling misinformation to reach millions, often without accountability or fact-checking. Algorithms reinforce biases by amplifying content aligned with users' pre-existing beliefs, making it even harder to correct falsehoods. This creates an urgent need for individuals to develop critical thinking skills, evaluate sources, and become more discerning information consumers, empowering them to resist manipulation and misinformation.

Addressing misinformation helps restore trust in institutions like media, science, and government, which is essential for societal cohesion. It promotes accountability and higher standards of accuracy, fostering confidence in public discourse. Confronting falsehoods also has an ethical dimension; sharing accurate information is a collective responsibility, as failing to address falsehoods allows them to persist and cause harm.

By tackling misinformation, we promote a culture of honesty, accountability, and reason, which benefits all aspects of society. Efforts to combat misinformation should include:

- Fact-checking

- Engaging in respectful conversations to dispel myths.

- Advocating for platform accountability.

- Amplifying well-researched information to counterbalance the reach of falsehoods.

These actions protect individual understanding and ensure a society built on trust, reason, and informed decision-making.

A friend of mine once posted a statement on social media. I asked if he had fact-checked his statement. He said he didn't trust fact-checkers. That response has haunted me for years. It stresses the importance of our due diligence when determining whether we discern the truth or a lie.

There are several reasons why some individuals may not find the truth helpful or desirable and might prefer to believe a lie. For some, the truth can be uncomfortable or threatening because it challenges deeply held beliefs or disrupts their worldview.

Accepting the truth may require people to confront complex realities about themselves, their choices, or their circumstances, which can be emotionally overwhelming or destabilizing. Lies, conversely, can provide comfort, maintaining a sense of control or security by allowing individuals to avoid the cognitive dissonance that arises when reality clashes with their expectations or desires.

People may prefer lies because they offer a sense of belonging or identity. Group dynamics often reinforce shared narratives, even if they are false, because they foster solidarity and provide a common framework for understanding the world.

Rejecting those lies in favor of the truth could lead to alienation or rejection from one's community, which many people are unwilling to face. Lies can also be more appealing when they align with personal biases or aspirations, as they may validate one's opinions, choices, or emotions in a way the truth does not.

Practical concerns can also make lies seem more advantageous than the truth. The truth may require actions or changes that are difficult, costly, or inconvenient, while lies can justify inaction or provide an easier path forward. For example, denying a severe problem might temporarily relieve anxiety and avoid the burden of addressing it, even if this comes at the cost of long-term consequences. Additionally, lies can sometimes be deliberately chosen to protect oneself or others from pain, whether to shield someone's feelings, preserve a relationship, or avoid conflict.

On a broader societal level, some individuals or groups may prefer lies that serve their interests, such as reinforcing power dynamics, promoting an agenda, or maintaining a particular narrative that benefits them. The truth is unwelcome in these cases because it threatens to undermine those advantages. Ultimately, the preference for lies over truth is often rooted in human psychology, shaped by emotional, social, and practical factors that prioritize immediate comfort or gain over the discomfort or complexity that truth may bring.

Truth underpins everything, from personal integrity to the function of democracy. Understanding its importance helps us appreciate its power in upholding justice and trust. The harm caused by lies is well-documented, from personal betrayals to large-scale political scandals.

The harms caused by lies are documented across various fields of study and sectors, reflecting the multifaceted impact of falsehoods on individuals, societies, and institutions.

Psychological studies document the emotional and cognitive effects on individuals and relationships. Research shows that deception can lead to a loss of trust, anxiety, and emotional distress, particularly in personal and professional settings. Chronic exposure to lies, such as in manipulative relationships, has been linked to long-term mental health issues like depression or post-traumatic stress disorder. Behavioral experiments also reveal how lies can alter decision-making, perpetuate biases, and reinforce misinformation.

In journalism, the harms of lies are meticulously documented through investigations into misinformation, propaganda, and media manipulation. Scholars analyze how false news stories influence public opinion, create societal divisions, and undermine trust in media institutions. Case studies, such as the impact of misinformation campaigns during elections or health crises, provide concrete examples of lies affecting public discourse and policy decisions.

Political scientists examine the consequences of lies on governance and democracy. Studies document how misinformation can erode public trust in institutions, distort electoral processes, and enable authoritarianism. Historical analyses, such as those focusing on propaganda in totalitarian regimes or misinformation in political campaigns, highlight the societal and global impacts of lies in the political arena.

In health, lies' harms are well-documented in medical misinformation cases. Public health organizations and researchers record the consequences of false claims about vaccines, treatments, or diseases, including lower vaccination rates, the spread of preventable diseases, and increased mortality rates. For example, misinformation during the COVID-19 pandemic resulted in vaccine hesitancy and non-compliance with safety measures, exacerbating the crisis.

Legal records and criminological research document the harms of lies in contexts such as perjury, fraud, and defamation. Courts provide detailed case studies of how falsehoods can lead to wrongful convictions, financial losses, and reputational damage. Criminologists also study the role of deception in crimes like identity theft and scams, highlighting its economic and psychological toll on victims.

Sociological research explores how lies perpetuate stereotypes, maintain social hierarchies, and fuel discrimination. Cultural studies analyze the narratives and myths that sustain systemic inequalities, documenting their impact on marginalized communities. For instance, lies about historical events or cultural practices have been shown to reinforce prejudice and hinder social progress.

Economists document the financial consequences of lies in markets and organizations. Studies on fraud, insider trading, and false advertising reveal how deception undermines market integrity, erodes consumer confidence, and causes economic instability. For example, the global financial crisis of 2008 was partly attributed to systemic lies and misrepresentations within the financial industry.

Environmental studies well-document the consequences of lies about environmental issues, such as climate change denial or green-washing. False claims by corporations or interest groups can delay policy action, mislead the public, and exacerbate environmental degradation, with long-term implications for ecosystems and human survival.

Historians record the harms of lies in shaping public narratives and justifying harmful actions. From fabricated justifications for wars to the manipulation of historical records, lies have been shown to influence events with catastrophic consequences, such as the Holocaust or colonial exploitation (the practice of a dominant nation forcefully taking control of another country, primarily to exploit its people as cheap labor and its natural resources for economic gain, often with little benefit to the colonized population, essentially enriching the colonizing power at the expense of the colonized land and its people. (Wikipedia)).

In the digital age, researchers in technology and cybersecurity document the harms caused by online lies, such as deepfakes, phishing schemes (a cybercrime where attackers send deceptive emails, texts, or messages that appear to be from a legitimate source to trick users into revealing sensitive information like passwords, credit card numbers, or social security numbers by clicking malicious links or providing details on fake websites designed to steal their data), and misinformation on social media. These studies highlight the societal risks of unchecked digital deception, including its potential to destabilize democracies and erode trust in digital communication.

The harms caused by lies are extensively documented in these fields through empirical research, case studies, and historical analysis, providing a robust understanding of their wide-ranging effects. This body of work serves as a foundation for developing strategies to mitigate the impact of deception and promote truth in public and private life.

Developing a critical lens when consuming information is essential for recognizing and resisting manipulative tactics because it equips individuals with the skills to evaluate the accuracy, intent, and credibility of the information they encounter. Manipulative tactics, such as emotional appeals, selective framing, or outright falsehoods, are designed to exploit cognitive biases and influence opinions, often without the recipient realizing it. A critical lens allows individuals to pause, question, and analyze the content they are exposed to rather than accepting it at face value.

A critical lens helps individuals identify biased or unreliable sources. Manipulative tactics often involve cherry-picking facts, using misleading headlines, or presenting opinions as facts. By critically assessing the credibility of sources, cross-referencing claims, and identifying potential conflicts of interest, individuals can discern whether the information is trustworthy or intended to mislead. This skill is essential in the digital age, where anyone can publish content online, and misinformation spreads rapidly.

Critical thinking also enables people to recognize emotional manipulation. Propaganda, political rhetoric, and even advertisements frequently appeal to emotions like fear, anger, or hope to bypass logical reasoning and provoke knee-jerk reactions. A critical lens helps individuals distinguish between emotional appeals that inform and those that manipulate, allowing them to respond thoughtfully rather than impulsively.

Another critical lens development aspect is understanding logical fallacies and rhetorical devices. Manipulative tactics often rely on flawed reasoning, such as false dichotomies, ad hominem attacks, or strawman arguments. Recognizing these techniques empowers individuals to deconstruct arguments and identify weaknesses, ensuring they are not swayed by illogical or deceptive reasoning.

A critical lens fosters skepticism toward sensationalism and over-simplified narratives. Manipulative tactics thrive on exaggerating claims or reducing complex issues to black-and-white terms. Critical thinkers seek context, question missing perspectives, and challenge overly simplistic explanations, enabling them to arrive at a more nuanced and accurate understanding.

Developing a critical lens cultivates an awareness of personal biases and how they can be exploited. Manipulative tactics often reinforce pre-existing beliefs or appeal to identity, making it easier for misinformation to take hold. By reflecting on their biases, individuals can approach information more objectively and avoid being manipulated by content that aligns too conveniently with their views.

Developing a critical lens transforms individuals into active participants in the information process rather than passive consumers. This empowerment protects them from manipulation and contributes to a more informed and discerning society capable of holding information sources accountable and resisting the spread of harmful misinformation.

By showing the consequences of dishonesty, I want to demonstrate how deception can lead to societal breakdown, distrust, and long-term damage. I'll also address people's moral dilemmas when choosing between truth and falsehood, helping us reflect on our values and decisions.

Historical examples of lies and their effects show dishonesty's far-reaching impact on nations and lives. Through a historical lens, we can see how truth shapes events. Lies are a personal failing and a force that alters societies. In today's media landscape, manipulation is a powerful tool. Developing a critical lens when consuming information is essential to see through manipulative tactics.

In today's digital age, unverified information spreads rapidly, eroding trust in institutions and relationships. This proliferation highlights the urgent need to foster a culture of truth and accountability. Without it, unethical practices and injustices thrive, leaving society vulnerable.

For young people, critical thinking and media literacy are essential tools to navigate misinformation and build informed perspectives. Globally, understanding how cultures perceive truth enriches dialogue and reduces conflict. Upholding truth as a cornerstone of justice requires education, transparency, and accountability. Empowering individuals to engage with information critically can create a more trustworthy, ethical, and connected world for future generations.

The ethical dilemmas around truth and falsehood challenge us to think deeply about morality. Cognitive biases often cloud our judgment, leading us to believe false information. By recognizing existing biases, we gain tools for truth-seeking.

Valuing truthfulness leads to personal growth and brings about societal benefits. It builds trust, strengthens relationships, and fosters more profound connections with others. A personal commitment to honesty leads to a fulfilling and authentic life. On a societal level, it contributes to a just and trustworthy community. Recognizing these benefits inspires us to prioritize truth in our interactions and decisions.

People have always lied, from small personal deceptions to more extensive manipulations for power or gain. However, social media has amplified the scale and impact of lying. Platforms enable lies to spread instantly to millions, making it easier to fabricate stories, manipulate facts, or create misleading personas.

The anonymity and reach of the digital world blur accountability, leaving many unaware of the harm lies can cause such as damaged reputations, broken trust, and societal division. While lying is often considered harmless, its long-term effects can be devastating. The question remains: do people genuinely grasp the far-reaching consequences of dishonesty in the digital age?

Bias is a natural cognitive tendency that shapes how we perceive the world, often rooted in our upbringing, experiences, cultural norms, and survival instincts. While it helps us make quick decisions, bias can distort truth and fairness, leading to misjudgments, prejudice, and systemic inequalities. Recognizing its origins is the first step toward controlling it.

To manage bias, individuals and institutions must embrace self-awareness and education. Identifying personal blind spots through introspection, feedback, or training can reveal hidden prejudices. Exposure to diverse perspectives, cultures, and viewpoints fosters empathy and challenges ingrained assumptions. Organizations can implement structured decision- making processes, reducing reliance on subjective judgments. Encouraging data-driven approaches and critical thinking ensures a more balanced assessment of information.

Technology, such as artificial intelligence, also plays a dual role.

While it can perpetuate bias when algorithms reflect human prejudices, it can equally help identify and mitigate biases in hiring, content moderation, and other areas.

Should we strive to eliminate bias? The answer is nuanced. Some biases, like a preference for safety or affinity toward loved ones, are vital for human connection and well-being. However, biases that distort the truth, promote inequity or hinder justice must be addressed. Striving for fairness doesn't mean erasing individuality but ensuring that principles of equity, truth, and respect guide our judgments and decisions.

Controlling harmful biases creates a foundation for truth, justice, and a more inclusive society where individuals can thrive without fear of misrepresentation or discrimination.

Science's quest for truth through empirical evidence exemplifies humanity's desire to understand the world. By highlighting the role of truth in science and contrasting it with pseudoscience and conspiracy theories, I hope others will adopt evidence-based thinking. This understanding of truth is essential and is the foundation of a functioning democracy. Lies and misinformation undermine democratic processes, leading to misinformed citizens and corrupt governance. Advocating for truth in political discourse is crucial for the health of our democratic institutions. Dishonesty has profound legal implications.

Embracing truthfulness and integrity, both personally and professionally, promotes transparency. Our advocacy for truth in political discourse is crucial for the well-being of democracy. Philosophers have long debated the nature of truth, and exploring their perspectives deepens the conversation about reality.

In a world where fake news is increasingly prevalent, developing tools to recognize and counter it is necessary. Learning to identify and debunk false stories is essential to building resilience against misinformation, and by being vigilant and prepared, we can all contribute to a more truthful public discourse. Truth-telling improves communication, strengthens relationships, and resolves conflicts.

References

American Press Institute The role of journalism in combating misinformation and supporting democratic discourse. Retrieved from: https://www.americanpressinstitute.org.

American Psychological Association (APA) Psychological effects of misinformation and the importance of fostering media literacy. Retrieved from: https://www.apa.org.

FactCheck.org Fighting false information: Tools and strategies for political accountability. Retrieved from: https://www.factcheck.org.

Journal of Applied Research in Memory and Cognition, 6(4), 353-369. DOI: 10.1016/j-jarmac. 2017.07.008.

Lewandowsky, S., Ecker, U. K., & Cook, J. (2017) Beyond misinformation: Coping strategies in the "post-truth" era.

PolitiFact Fact-checking in the digital age: Tools for navigating misinformation. Retrieved from: https://www.politifact.com.

Snopes Strategies for identifying misinformation on social media and news platforms. Retrieved from: https://www.snopes.com.

Stanford History Education Group (SHEG) (2019) Evaluating online sources: Building civic and critical reasoning skills. Retrieved from: https://sheg.stanford.edu.

Wardle, C., & Derakhshan, H. (2017) Information Disorder: Toward an Interdisciplinary Framework for Research and Policymaking. Council of Europe. Retrieved from: https://www.coe.int.

World Economic Forum (2023) Tackling the global infodemic: Strategies for media, policymakers, and citizens. Retrieved from: https://www.weforum.org.

Zuckerman, E. (2021) Mistrust: Why Losing Faith in Institutions Provides the Tools to Transform Them. New York: W. W. Norton & Company.

Chapter Two:
Cultural Differences in Perspective

Values, norms, language, and historical context influence cultural perspectives on truth and untruth. In some cultures, honesty is a virtue; in others, the 'white lies' concept is acceptable. Some cultures highlight the moral implications of lying, while others view it as a necessary social tool. In East Asia, for example, people value truth to maintain harmony. Withholding truths or telling small lies might be acceptable if it avoids conflict or protects relationships. Individualist cultures, like the United States and Western Europe, value personal honesty and transparency even if it leads to discomfort or conflict, seeing truth as an individual responsibility.

Evidence suggests that cultural attitudes toward honesty vary significantly across societies. In cultures like those of Scandinavia and Germany, honesty is often regarded as a core virtue, tied to values such as trust, transparency, and individual accountability. In these societies, even small untruths can be viewed as breaches of integrity. Conversely, in cultures such as Japan or many parts of East Asia, white lies—often considered "benevolent deception"— are more acceptable and may even be encouraged to preserve social harmony or avoid embarrassing others.

Studies in cross-cultural psychology, such as those examining the Social Orientations Framework, reveal that collectivist cultures often prioritize relational harmony over strict truth-telling, while individualistic cultures value directness and factual accuracy. Anthropological fieldwork and surveys, like those from the World Values Survey, further highlight these differing norms, illustrating how each cultural context shapes its approach to honesty.

Communication styles are essential in understanding what is said and what others mean. In high-context cultures, communication is through non-verbal cues or shared understanding. Japan or Middle Eastern countries may use subtlety in truth-telling, leaving much unsaid but understood based on the context.

Clear and explicit communication in low-context cultures, such as Germany or the United States, view indirectness as evasive or dishonest. Western cultures generally prioritize confrontation, even at the risk of embarrassment, with less emphasis on saving face. Cultural views on the morality of lying also differ.

Some societies see through a practical lens, where the ends justify the means. Lying to protect someone from harm may be considered morally acceptable if it serves the greater good. In contrast, many Western cultures, especially those influenced by Christian or Kantian philosophies, often hold that lying is wrong regardless of the outcome. In these views, truth is an absolute moral value. Religious and spiritual beliefs further shape cultural views on truth. Truth links to righteousness in Abrahamic religions like Christianity, Islam, and Judaism. It is a fundamental virtue, like protecting life.

Kantian philosophy has influenced the ethical and political thinking of many Western countries, particularly those in Europe and North America. While no country explicitly "follows" Kantian philosophy in its entirety, his ideas have shaped the moral and legal frameworks of nations such as Germany (where Kant was born), and his emphasis on human dignity, autonomy, and universal principles is reflected in international human rights laws, including those promoted by institutions like the United Nations. In countries like the United States, Canada, and much of Western Europe, Kant's ideas on individual rights, justice, and equality have influenced legal systems, particularly in constitutional law, human rights discourse, and discussions about ethical governance. However, Kantian ethics is just one strand of philosophical influence, and many other moral frameworks coexist within these countries.

Kantian philosophy emphasizes that moral actions must be guided by universal principles derived from reason, where individuals act out of duty rather than personal desires or consequences. Central to this is the categorical imperative, which demands that one act only according to maxims that could be universally applied, treating others as ends in themselves and never merely as means to an end.

Viewing truth and lies through a practical lens means evaluating honesty or deception based on their outcomes or utility rather than rigid moral absolutes. In cultures with this perspective, the decision to tell the truth or a lie depends on its practical consequences—whether it helps achieve a desirable goal, maintain social harmony, or prevent harm. For example, in many collectivist societies, a lie might be deemed acceptable if it spares someone embarrassment, preserves relationships, or avoids conflict. This approach considers the context and potential impact of truth-telling or lying, prioritizing pragmatic benefits like emotional well-being, societal stability, or efficient problem-solving over strict adherence to an abstract principle of honesty.

In other cultures, truth is less about literal accuracy and more about conveying cultural wisdom through myths or storytelling. Legal and political systems reflect cultural attitudes toward truth. In Western legal systems, truth is essential for justice. People punish lying. Legal and political systems often mirror cultural values, with Western legal systems emphasizing truth as fundamental to justice, ensuring fairness through evidence and testimony. In these systems, lying is considered a serious offense, punishable through laws against perjury, fraud, and obstruction of justice, reflecting the belief that truth underpins societal trust and order.

In some non-Western legal systems, the emphasis may be on reconciliation and maintaining harmony. Historical and political contexts can further complicate perceptions of truth. In societies that have experienced war, colonialism, or authoritarian rule, official narratives might be untrustworthy. People may rely on coded language or subtext to understand what is   true. When people rely on coded language or subtext to understand what is true, they interpret implied meanings or indirect communication rather than explicit statements. This often occurs in cultures or situations where directness is avoided to maintain politeness, navigate power dynamics, or express sensitive truths in a socially acceptable way.

In business, cultural norms around truth-telling can differ. In some regions, such as parts of the Middle East and China, truth can be flexible in negotiations, with strategic exaggeration or omission seen as acceptable. In cultures like the United States or Germany, directness and transparency in business dealings are essential for building trust and maintaining long-term relationships. In some cultures, politeness may precede blunt honesty in social interactions. In Japan, people might downplay lousy news to avoid offense. At the same time, the Netherlands and Israel value it even if it risks being rude. Cultures vary in their tolerance for ambiguity.

Examining the differences between truth and untruth across cultures requires understanding what high-context and low-context cultures mean. High-context and low-context cultures describe how people communicate within different cultural environments. Both types of communication, high-context, and low-context, reflect the broader social norms of each culture. Understanding these cultural nuances is critical to effective cross- cultural communication. This topic of exploring cultural views on truth and lies is ideal for those interested in cross-cultural studies, ethics, or social psychology, including students, educators, and professionals in anthropology, sociology, or international relations. This topic appeals to a general audience curious about how cultural norms shape communication, relationships, and legal or political systems worldwide.

Across the world, societies have developed diverse cultural norms rooted in their historical, environmental, and social contexts, which influence how truth is valued and expressed. In individualistic societies, like many in the West, truth often emerges as a key moral and practical principle tied to personal accountability and the functioning of legal systems, where honesty ensures trust and justice. Conversely, in collectivist societies, truth is frequently balanced with considerations of harmony and relational dynamics, leading to a nuanced approach where preserving group cohesion may sometimes take precedence over strict factual accuracy.

In high context cultures, communication relies heavily on the surrounding context, including nonverbal cues, relationships, social norms, and shared experiences, with the expectation that meaning without spelling it out is understood. Prioritizing relationships and social harmony reflect an indirect communication style relying on nonverbal cues and shared understanding. Characteristics include indirect communication and rely on reading between the lines. Expected behavior includes non-verbal cues, gestures, tone, and facial expressions to maintain harmony, avoid conflict, and "save face." Shared backgrounds or experiences reduce the need for explanations.

Low context cultures include individual responsibility and transparent information exchange. Directness, with clear communication leaving little room for interpretation, is valued. Communication is direct and uses precise language with little reliance on the surrounding context to understand meaning. Individuals say what they mean and ensure clarity over subtlety. There is less reliance on non-verbal cues. Misunderstanding lessens because communication is explicit. Unambiguous communication is standard. The focus is on logical and information over relationships. Verbal expression and handling conflict and disagreement through direct discussion are priorities.

Understanding and appreciating the many aspects of cultural diversity are essential for effective cross-cultural communication. A conversation might include many implied meanings, and people may feel uncomfortable with blunt or overly direct communication, especially in sensitive situations. While truth and untruth are universal concepts, their application varies significantly across cultures. Cultural sensitivity is helpful when navigating these differences. Being deceptive in one culture might be considered virtuous in another. Following are examples of how a few primary world cultures view truth and untruth.

The United States (North America) is a low-context, individualistic society emphasizing transparency and personal honesty. Telling the truth, even if uncomfortable, is valued. Straightforwardness and factual accuracy are essential in business, whereas "white lies" are less accepted than in collectivist cultures.

Brazil (South America) is a high-context and collectivist society where relationships and social harmony are crucial in communication. People might use indirect or diplomatic approaches to avoid conflict or maintain a pleasant atmosphere. Truth is secondary to maintaining good relationships, especially in business dealings.

In Japan (East Asia), someone might express disapproval simply through silence or subtle body language rather than directly saying "no." Japan's high-context and collectivist culture nuances are true. Managing confrontation avoids harmony and "saves face."

In China (East Asia), a collectivist society, truth-telling is shaped by the need to maintain social harmony. Lying or withholding information may be acceptable if it protects family, community, or relationships. Strategic exaggeration or omission in negotiations is a standard part of the process.

The communication style in India (South Asia) can vary across its diverse cultures. It is high context where indirect communication is standard. Religious or spiritual values may justify flexible truths. Portraying truth as situational, depending on moral and contextual factors, is evidenced in Hindu epics like the Mahabharata.

Saudi Arabia (Middle East) is a high-context culture with solid religious influences that value truth-telling within the framework of Islamic principles. Honesty is essential but preserving honor and "saving face" is also important.

Saudi Arabians may use tactful omissions or indirect truths to avoid offense or embarrassment in business or social contexts.

Germany (Western Europe) is a low-context culture and values direct, clear communication. Truth is explicit, with a high emphasis on factual accuracy and reliability. In professional settings, for example, contracts and agreements are expected to be precise, and ambiguity is discouraged.

France (Western Europe) is a low-context culture where intellectual debate and honesty in discussions are highly valued. French communication can also be nuanced, focusing on diplomacy and tact. Truth in business and social interactions is precise. Sensitivity to context is appreciated.

Russia (Eastern European) is a high context communication style that relies on subtext and reading between the lines. Suspicion of truth in social and political contexts is common, especially given historical experiences with authoritarian rule. People emphasize loyalty and may withhold truths to protect those they trust.

Australia (Oceania) maintains a low context, individualistic culture favoring straightforward communication. Honesty and openness are appreciated, and "telling it like it is" is a common expectation in business and social settings. The style in Australia, a laid-back, egalitarian attitude, finds excessive bluntness rude.

South Africa (Sub-Saharan Africa) believes maintaining communal harmony is often more important than strict adherence to individual truths. In rural and urban settings, indirect communication and "saving face" can influence how truth is handled, with people often prioritizing group well-being over blunt honesty.

In Nigeria (West Africa), a high-context culture, truth is usually viewed as communal and familial relationships. Honesty is valued, but indirectness maintains respect or avoids conflict. Elders may not share brutal truths with younger people to protect their emotional well-being or preserve family cohesion.

Exposure to different cultural perspectives in our workplace, neighborhoods, and schools fosters creativity. Each of us brings unique ideas shaped by our backgrounds, which leads to innovative solutions and new ways of thinking. Living with diverse cultures promotes understanding and empathy.

Considering other viewpoints enhances our interpersonal relationships and improves communication and collaboration. Individuals who experience a multicultural environment become more adaptable, open-minded, and better prepared to navigate cross-cultural interactions in a globalized world.

As we work with people from other cultures in our workplace, neighborhoods, and schools, understanding cultural differences in telling and dealing with truth and untruths becomes essential in our sensitivity to communication. Recognizing how we communicate and its impact on others requires accepting various perspectives. We have opportunities to learn and adapt to differences as we work and live with diverse individuals. We can expand our ability to function with many aspects of cultural diversity, which is essential for effective cross-cultural communication.

References

Beer, J. E. (2003). Communicating across cultures. Retrieved from http://www.culture-at-work.com/highlow.html

Hofstede Insights. (n.d.). Japan. Retrieved from https://www.hofstede-insights.com/country-comparison/japan/

Moran, T., Abramson, N. R., & Moran, S. V. (2014). Managing cultural differences (9th ed.). Oxford: Routledge.

Penn State University. (n.d.). High-context and low-context cultures.

Chapter Three:
Telling Truth from Fiction

On August 25, 1835, the New York Sun published the first of six articles claiming the discovery of life on the moon, later known as "The Great Moon Hoax." These articles, allegedly reprinted from the Edinburgh Journal of Science, were attributed to Dr. Andrew Grant, a fictional colleague of the famous astronomer Sir John Herschel. Herschel traveled to Capetown, South Africa, in 1834 to set up an observatory with a powerful telescope. The article falsely reported that he had discovered life on the moon, including unicorns, two-legged beavers, and bat-like humanoids.

Upon its publication, the first moon hoax article in the New York Sun, a 'penny press' paper established in 1833, sparked a surge in sales. The engaging style of journalism and the sensational content attracted a broad audience even though the entire story was a fabrication. The Edinburgh Journal of Science had ceased publication years earlier. Dr. Grant was an invented character. The articles were likely written by Sun reporter Richard Adams Locke, a Cambridge-educated journalist, as a satirical commentary on earlier speculative theories about extraterrestrial life, particularly those of Reverend Thomas Dick, who claimed the moon had 4.2 billion inhabitants.

Despite its satirical intent, the story fooled many, including a group of Yale University scientists who traveled to New York searching for the original Edinburgh Journal articles. After being misled by Sun employees, the scientists returned to New Haven. On September 16, 1835, the Sun confessed that the articles were a hoax, but the revelation didn't harm the paper's popularity. The Sun continued publishing until it merged with the New York World-Telegram in 1950. The merger dissolved in 1967. The New York Sun newspaper was established in 2002, though unrelated to the original.

This story illustrates several important lessons about why people might believe lies. When information comes from a seemingly credible source, like a reputable newspaper or a supposed expert, people are more likely to accept it as accurate. The New York Sun established itself as a famous paper, and the use of Sir John Herschel's name, a respected astronomer, lent an air of legitimacy to the hoax. The New York Sun's moon hoax, with its sensational claims of life on the moon, tapped into the public's imagination and curiosity about the unknown. The idea of a moon teeming with life, complete with fantastical creatures and lush landscapes, portrayed an adventure.

When many people believe something, it can create a bandwagon effect, and others are more likely to accept it. The widespread acceptance of the moon hoax likely reinforced belief in the story. The moon hoax is a cautionary tale that highlights the importance of critical thinking. Readers should have questioned the story's validity or recognized it as satire, demonstrating how easily persuasive narratives can sway people without engaging in critical thinking or seeking to verify information. People are likely to believe information that aligns with their beliefs or desires. The fascination with the possibility of extraterrestrial life made people more receptive to the hoax.

The story highlights how satire or fiction can be mistaken for fact, particularly when it does not identify as such. This misinterpretation can lead to widespread misinformation. The "Great Moon Hoax" did not seem to have any lasting effects on the credibility of the New York Sun newspaper, as the paper continued publishing and remained popular despite the confession of the hoax. The widespread belief in the moon hoax raised questions about the credibility and trustworthiness of the media. It demonstrated the potential for unchecked sensationalism to influence public opinion. It highlighted the importance of critically evaluating information from the press.

The "Great Moon Hoax" significantly impacted public perception of scientific discoveries and journalism at that time, raising questions about the credibility of scientific information and journalistic sources. This event highlighted the importance of critical thinking and skepticism when evaluating extraordinary claims. It underscored the potential consequences of unchecked sensationalism in the media. The widespread belief in the fabricated articles claiming the discovery of life on the moon demonstrated the public's susceptibility to sensational and unverified claims.

The "Great Moon Hoax" teaches us to be cautious and critical of emotionally charged language, check the source's credibility, and recognize when we are in a filter bubble or echo chamber. These quick and practical tools can help us improve our media literacy and determine who is behind the information, where the evidence comes from, and whether it is in the proper context.

After the 1938 radio broadcast of H.G. Wells' War of the Worlds, adapted by Orson Welles, widespread panic allegedly erupted as some listeners believed the fictional alien invasion was real. The broadcast's realistic news bulletin style, combined with the tense global atmosphere on the brink of World War II, led many to miss the disclaimers identifying it as a drama. While reports of chaos, such as people fleeing homes or jamming police lines, were likely exaggerated by the press, the incident highlighted the power of mass media to influence public perception and sparked debates about media responsibility and audience gullibility.

The 1874 New York Zoo Hoax: On November 9, 1874, the New York Herald published a fabricated front-page article claiming that animals had escaped from the Central Park Zoo and were rampaging through the city, resulting in numerous deaths and injuries. The article caused widespread panic among readers before it was revealed to be a hoax intended to critique the zoo's safety measures.

The 1983 Chilean Earthquake and Tsunami Hoax: In 1983, a false prediction circulated in Chile, claiming that a massive earthquake and tsunami would devastate the country. The hoax led to widespread fear and unnecessary evacuations, highlighting the impact of misinformation on public behavior.

The 2012 Mayan Calendar Apocalypse: Leading up to December 21, 2012, widespread belief emerged that the Mayan calendar predicted the end of the world on that date. Media coverage and sensationalism fueled global anxiety, prompting survival preparations and even drastic actions, despite experts clarifying that the calendar marked a transition, not a doomsday event.

We live in a world where "information is coming at us, as opposed to us looking for information," said Annie Zeidman-Karpinski, the Ken and Kenda Singer Science Librarian at the University of Oregon. "We were given tools for a different era of media. Tools that were more effective when media was simpler." How can you tell if what you are reading is factual? When you read information, ask yourself who is behind the information, what the evidence is, and what other sources say.

"SIFT provides a framework for thinking about what we can do to investigate some of these fundamental questions," said Zeidman-Karpinski. SIFT stands for Stop. Investigate the source. Find better coverage. Trace the claims, quotes, and media back to their original context. When we read a story online, the overall context is often missing. We need to "trace it back to find out if you understand the context correctly," Zeidman-Karpinski explained. A complementary technique used with SIFT is lateral reading. Click links, open new windows, or start new searches to verify the claims in an article. Trace them to the primary source or do further research on the topic.

References

Digital Inquiry Group
https://cor.inquirygroup.org/curriculum/collections/a-little-of-everything/

A 3-minute video from the University Libraries at the University of Louisville shows how fact-checkers use lateral reading of websites to evaluate news sources. The key message is to move throughout the Web to assess the website. Do not rely solely on the content or links of the website itself ("vertical reading").
https://researchguides.uoregon.edu/fakenews/lateral_reading

When evaluating a source on the Web, don't just look at the source. Some sites may look professional and credible but promote a specific agenda or viewpoint. It's always a good idea to open a new tab and do a web search on the source and/or the organization that is providing it.

These short online videos from Mike Caulfield at Washington State University provide a good introduction:

https://www.youtube.com/watch?v=yBU2sDlUbp8

https://www.youtube.com/watch?v=hB6qjIxKltA

https://www.youtube.com/watch?v=tRZ-N3OvvUs

https://www.youtube.com/watch?v=wJG7kFmS0FE&t=151s

https://www.history.com/this-day-in-history/the-great-moon-hoax

Quick tips for telling the truth from fiction online – Oregon Health News Blog.https://covidblog.oregon.gov/quick-tips-for-telling-truth-from-fiction-online/

Chapter Four:
Why People Lie

Lying is an integral part of human interaction, often used to navigate social situations tactfully or deceptively. Lies can range from harmless "white lies" trying to spare someone's feelings to more damaging forms of deceit with consequences. Understanding the difference between these forms of lying and knowing when it may be acceptable to bend the truth is essential in maintaining healthy relationships and social harmony.

Examples of White Lies

1. **Complimenting a Friend's Outfit:** Telling a friend, "You look great in that outfit!" even if you think it's not their best look. This lie spares their feelings and boosts their confidence without causing harm.

2. **Enjoying a Gift:** Expressing excitement about a gift received you don't like by saying, "This is what I wanted!" The lie shows appreciation for the thoughtfulness of the gift-giver.

3. **Pretending to Enjoy a Meal:** Complimenting a home-cooked meal with, "This is delicious!" even if it's not to your taste. This lie avoids making the cook feel bad and keeps the atmosphere pleasant.

Examples of Harmful Lies

1. **Lying about Financial Stability:** Telling a spouse or partner that everything is fine financially when debt is mounting. This lie prevents open communication and can lead to severe relationship and financial issues.

2. **False Medical Expertise:** Claiming you're knowledgeable about health conditions to a friend seeking advice when you need more proper understanding. This lie can mislead someone into making uninformed decisions about their health.

3. **Undermining a Colleague:** Spreading rumors about a colleague's performance or character at work to tarnish their reputation. This lie

can harm their career and damage the work environment for everyone involved.

There is a significant difference between these harmless fibs and more harmful lies used to cover up faults, avoid responsibility, or manipulate others. Lies in close relationships, like those between spouses or close friends, can cause lasting harm if they break trust, and restoring that trust is often challenging.

Trust is a foundation built over time through honesty, vulnerability, and consistency, and even a small lie can create cracks that undermine its strength. When lies reveal themselves, feelings of betrayal, insecurity, and doubt can surface, making it difficult for both parties to feel safe in the relationship. Rebuilding trust requires patience, transparency, and a commitment to honest communication—an emotional labor that, while possible, often demands significant time and effort from both individuals involved.

In professional settings, dishonesty can be career-ending, as most workplaces highly value integrity. Lies meant to deceive rather than protect often damage relationships and reputations in ways that are hard to mend. When an employee lies, it disrupts workflow and erodes the trust of colleagues, supervisors, and clients. Lies intended to deceive rather than protect can lead to questions about an individual's reliability and ethics, casting doubt on their entire work and judgment.

In competitive or high-stakes environments, even a single instance of dishonesty can overshadow achievements, limit future opportunities, and damage one's professional reputation. Once trust is lost, colleagues may hesitate to collaborate, and superiors may withhold essential responsibilities, making it challenging to regain footing in the organization.

Lying can take an emotional toll, as even the smallest untruths can weigh on the conscience, fostering stress and anxiety. This internal tension grows as individuals brace for the potential exposure of the truth, creating a lingering sense of unease and insecurity. Reflecting on the intention behind a lie can offer valuable guidance in deciding whether honesty is the better path. If telling the truth can help someone grow, improve, or address a personal challenge, choosing honesty may be the more compassionate and supportive approach.

Conversely, when a lie is a way to sidestep responsibility or avoid discomfort rather than genuinely protect another's feelings, opting for honesty can reflect tremendous respect for the other person and oneself—moreover, placing oneself in the other person's position and imagining how one would feel if the roles were reversed can be revealing. This exercise in empathy helps clarify whether a lie is justified as kindness or merely a convenient escape, ultimately guiding us toward choices that align with our values and foster more profound, more genuine connections.

Frequent lying is often a coping mechanism for those who fear confrontation, seek social acceptance, or crave validation, particularly among teenagers who may feel pressure to conform or avoid rejection. For some, lying becomes a means of sidestepping uncomfortable situations, gaining approval, or masking insecurities, as the desire to be liked or to avoid judgment can drive them to say what they think others want to hear. However, when lying escalates into a compulsive behavior—often referred to as pathological lying—it goes beyond occasional, situational fibs and can cause significant harm.

Pathological lying, characterized by frequent and seemingly purposeless deception, is often deeply ingrained, and can lead to a breakdown in relationships, as friends, family, and colleagues may struggle to trust someone who lies compulsively. The impact of pathological lying extends to the individual as well, as it can lead to intense feelings of guilt, shame, and isolation.

This behavior is often symptomatic of underlying psychological issues and may require professional intervention to help the person recognize and address the roots of their dishonesty. In such cases, therapy can play a critical role in uncovering the underlying motivations for compulsive lying and developing healthier, more transparent ways of interacting with others, ultimately fostering more robust and trusting relationships.

Lying is inevitable in human interactions, but understanding when it's appropriate and when it might cause harm is critical. White lies may be necessary to maintain social harmony, but honesty should be prioritized in meaningful relationships. If lying becomes a habitual way to sidestep issues, it's worthwhile to reflect on one's motivations or seek guidance. Ultimately, while the truth is not always easy, it remains the foundation of trust, and knowing when to tell it is a valuable skill for maintaining healthy relationships and a clear conscience.

Acknowledging that lying is an inevitable part of human interactions significantly impacts how we assess the truth. This realization prompts a more nuanced approach to communication, trust, and the evaluation of information.

Understanding that deception can occur even in everyday conversations encourages us to develop critical thinking skills. We become more cautious about accepting information at face value, prompting us to seek evidence, verify sources, and consider alternative perspectives. This heightened skepticism can protect us from misinformation but may also lead to over-cautiousness or distrust if not balanced properly.

Recognizing that not all lies are equal helps us assess the truth more effectively. Some lies, often termed "white lies," are used to protect feelings or maintain social harmony. By understanding the context and intent behind a statement, we can better judge its veracity and significance. This means paying attention to cues like tone, body language, and situational factors that might influence why someone chooses to be less than truthful.

The inevitability of lying affects how we build and maintain trust. Knowing that deception is possible, we might place greater emphasis on transparency and open communication to establish reliable relationships. This can lead to setting clear expectations and boundaries about honesty in personal and professional interactions.

Understanding when lying is appropriate versus harmful forces us to confront ethical dilemmas. It requires us to weigh the consequences of truth versus deception in each situation. This moral calculus impacts how we perceive others' honesty and how we choose to act, influencing societal norms around integrity and responsibility.

Being aware of the potential for dishonesty shapes our communication methods. We might employ more direct questioning, seek corroboration from multiple sources, or use technology to verify information. This proactive approach aims to reduce misunderstandings and uncover the truth more efficiently.

Assessing truth in the context of inevitable lying also involves understanding human emotions and motivations. Developing emotional intelligence allows us to empathize with others, recognize why they might choose to lie, and address underlying issues such as fear, embarrassment, or pressure.

The inevitability of lying in human interactions necessitates a balanced and thoughtful approach to assessing the truth. By considering context, intent, and potential impact, we can navigate deception more effectively. This perspective encourages the development of critical thinking, ethical judgment, and emotional intelligence, ultimately leading to more honest and meaningful interactions.

References

American Psychological Association. (n.d.). Pathological lying: Symptoms and implications. Retrieved from https://www.apa.org

Bok, S. (1999). Lying: Moral choice in public and private life. New York, NY: Vintage Books.

DePaulo, B. M., & Kashy, D. A. (1998). Every day lies in close and casual relationships. Journal of Personality and Social Psychology, 74(1), 63–79. https://doi.org/10.1037/0022-3514.74.1.63

Ekman, P. (2009). Telling lies: Clues to deceit in the marketplace, politics, and marriage (4th ed.). New York, NY: W.W. Norton & Company.

Goleman, D. (1995). Emotional intelligence: Why it can matter more than IQ. New York, NY: Bantam Books.

Levine, T. R. (2014). Truth-default theory (TDT): A theory of human deception and deception detection. Journal of Language and Social Psychology, 33(4), 378–392. https://doi.org/10.1177/0261927X14535916

Maiese, M. (2006). Restorative justice. Beyond Intractability. Retrieved from https://www.beyondintractability.org

Vrij, A. (2008). Detecting lies and deceit: Pitfalls and opportunities (2nd ed.). Hoboken, NJ: Wiley.

Chapter Five:
Secret Societies

Global societies today refer to the interconnected and interdependent world communities formed due to globalization. They include diverse cultural, political, economic, and social systems that interact and influence each other across borders. As globalization accelerates, these societies have become more connected, creating opportunities and challenges in cultural exchange, economic interdependence, political cooperation, and technological connectivity. Additionally, global societies face shared challenges like climate change, health crises, and social inequality. Here, we'll explore the key aspects that define global societies and then analyze how secret societies, though traditionally operating in a concealed manner, relate to ideas of truth, deception, and their impact on everyday life.

Critical Aspects of Global Societies

The exchange of culture is one of the hallmarks of a global society. Through travel, media, migration, and technology, one culture's ideas, traditions, values, and practices reach others, creating a blend of cultural expressions. While leading to a shared global culture in some aspects, this process also allows unique cultural identities to be preserved. Examples include the international influence of foods like sushi or tacos and the spread of cultural celebrations like Diwali and Halloween. Despite blending, people worldwide retain their cultural heritage, creating multicultural societies.

Today's economies are highly interdependent, with local markets influenced by global supply chains, investments, and trade agreements. Multinational corporations and international financial institutions like the World Bank or International Monetary Fund play significant roles, creating economies where one country's success often impacts another. The reliance on international trade means that economic trends or crises in one part of the world, like the 2008 financial crash or the recent COVID-19 pandemic, can affect global markets.

Nationalism, defined as a political ideology that emphasizes the interests and culture of a particular nation, has experienced a notable resurgence in recent years. This trend is evident across various regions, including Europe, Asia, and the Americas, and is influenced by multiple factors:

Globalization has led to economic disparities, with certain communities feeling left behind. The outsourcing of jobs and the decline of local industries have fueled economic insecurities, prompting some to advocate for protectionist policies and a return to national economic sovereignty.

Increased immigration has introduced diverse cultures into traditionally homogeneous societies. This demographic shift has sparked debates over national identity, with some fearing the erosion of traditional values and customs. Such concerns have bolstered support for nationalist movements that prioritize preserving cultural heritage.

Leaders employing populist rhetoric have capitalized on public discontent by promoting nationalist agendas. They often position themselves as defenders of the "common people" against perceived threats from globalization and multiculturalism, thereby strengthening nationalist sentiments.

The rise of nationalism is not unprecedented. Historically, periods of significant social and economic change have often led to a resurgence of nationalist ideologies. For instance, the French Revolution and the Napoleonic Wars in the late 18th and early 19th centuries stimulated the rise of nationalism in Europe.

In Europe, countries like Hungary and Poland have witnessed the rise of nationalist parties that advocate for stricter immigration controls and the preservation of national sovereignty. In the United States, nationalist rhetoric has influenced policies on trade and immigration, reflecting a broader trend toward prioritizing national interests.

The current trend toward nationalism is a multifaceted phenomenon driven by economic insecurities, cultural identity concerns, populist political leadership, and historical precedents. Understanding these factors is crucial for comprehending the complexities of modern nationalist movements.

Political cooperation has become essential in addressing issues that transcend national boundaries, such as climate change, nuclear proliferation, and human rights. Organizations like the United Nations, European Union, and African Union bring countries together for collaborative efforts. However, these global interactions also give rise to political conflicts, often related to resource competition, power struggles, and ideological differences.

The spread of technology, particularly the internet and mobile communication, has bridged distances, allowing instant communication, global commerce, and knowledge exchange. This connectivity has fostered a sense of global citizenship, with people engaging in cross-border collaborations and discussions. While this connectivity has brought tremendous benefits, it has also led to challenges, including digital divides and privacy concerns.

Climate change, pandemics, and global inequality require collective action. From multinational organizations to grassroots NGOs (nonprofit organizations operating independently of any government, typically whose purpose is to address a social or political issue), stakeholders work together to tackle these issues. Climate action agreements, like the Paris Agreement or global health initiatives, are examples of these efforts. Yet, disparities in resources and power can complicate global responses, often creating tension between nations with different priorities or capacities.

People increasingly move across borders for work, education, or safety, resulting in multicultural societies. While migration adds to the cultural diversity of host countries, it also raises challenges, such as social integration, economic competition, and occasional xenophobia (dislike of or prejudice against people from other countries). However, as migration becomes a more common aspect of modern life, policies on integration and citizenship are evolving to reflect the needs of global societies.

In essence, global societies are characterized by complex and interdependent relationships, underscoring the importance of cooperation in addressing shared global issues while celebrating cultural diversity.

Secret Societies and Their Relationship to Truth and Lies

Secret societies have long intrigued the public, often seen as shadowy groups shrouded in mystery. Their relationship with truth and lies is shaped by the purpose, secrecy, and the public's perception of them. Here's how secret societies relate to truth, lies, and the tension between them.

Search for Higher Knowledge – Some societies claim to pursue hidden or higher truths, whether spiritual, philosophical, or esoteric. Freemasons or

Rosicrucians, for example, often seek enlightenment or self-improvement and a deeper understanding of life's mysteries.

Exclusive Knowledge – Secret societies frequently keep specific knowledge or rituals from outsiders. Members can justify this exclusivity to protect knowledge they believe is sacred or open only to those initiated.

Truth of Brotherhood – Many secret societies prioritize loyalty, trust, and shared ideals among members. This internal truth is inwardly focused, creating a sense of purpose and belonging for those within the society.

Deception and Secrecy – Secret societies often employ deception to protect their secrets and maintain their mystique. This may involve misleading outsiders or concealing their true intentions, leading to suspicion about these groups.

Conspiracy Theories – Secret societies are often linked to conspiracy theories, with the public sometimes viewing them as manipulative forces. Groups like the Illuminati are seen as controlling governments or economies secretly, even if these theories are largely speculative.

False Narratives and Myths – Some societies foster myths around their origins or goals to intrigue or confuse outsiders, maintaining an aura of mystery that allows them to operate without external interference.

Perception by Outsiders – For outsiders, the truth about secret societies is clouded by secrecy. This lack of transparency fuels distrust, as people still need help to determine whether the group's activities align with stated goals or if there are hidden motives.

Internal vs. External Truth – What secret society members consider truth may differ from what outsiders see. This duality creates a dynamic where truth and lies coexist, depending on perspective.

Examples of Real-Life Secret Societies and Their Impact

Throughout history, secret societies have captured the public's imagination, fueled by their rituals, symbols, and the perception that they wield hidden influence. While these organizations vary significantly in their goals and practices, they share a sense of exclusivity and mystery, inspiring countless theories, and debates. Below are ten real-life groups historically associated with secrecy or exclusivity. Each has its unique history and impact on society, contributing to the ongoing fascination with secret organizations.

The **Freemasons** are the most renowned secret society, dating back to the early 18th century. As a fraternal organization, Freemasonry is structured around elaborate rituals, symbols, and a hierarchical lodge system. Freemasons value personal development, moral uprightness, and brotherhood, with many famous leaders and influential figures counted among their members. While they are involved in charitable efforts worldwide, the organization's secretive nature and symbolic imagery, such as the compass and square, have led to widespread speculation about its influence on global politics, finance, and culture.

Founded in 1832 at Yale University, **Skull and Bones** is a highly exclusive student society with secretive membership and rituals. Many of its members come from prominent families and go on to hold influential positions in government, business, and finance. With a reputation for dark and mysterious initiation ceremonies, Skull and Bones has sparked speculation about its role in shaping the American elite. Alums include several U.S. presidents and influential leaders, which has only fueled the public's belief in its ability to influence national and international policies.

The **Bilderberg Group**, established in 1954, is a conference of influential political leaders, business executives, and intellectuals from North America and Europe. The group meets annually to discuss global economic and political issues in private, fueling suspicions that it acts as a shadowy organization guiding global policy. While not technically a secret society, the Bilderberg Group's closed-door meetings have inspired conspiracy theories about its intentions, with some believing it manipulates international events behind the scenes. Despite these claims, attendees assert that the discussions are informal and meant to encourage dialogue.

The **Illuminati** originally referred to as a Bavarian secret society founded in 1776 by Adam Weishaupt. This organization sought to promote Enlightenment ideals and challenge established authority but was banned shortly after its formation. Despite its brief existence, the concept of the Illuminati persists in modern conspiracy theories, with many believing that a reformed Illuminati controls world governments, economies, and media. The term has become a catch-all for a supposed hidden group that wields vast, unseen power, even though no credible evidence supports such an organization today.

Opus Dei, founded in 1928 by Spanish priest Josemaría Escrivá, is a Catholic prelature that integrates faith into daily life. Although not a secret society, its strict practices, hierarchical structure, and conservative stance on religious doctrine have aroused public curiosity and suspicion. Members of Opus Dei are known for their deep commitment to spiritual discipline, sometimes practicing physical mortification as a form of devotion. While critics question its influence within the Catholic Church, especially following its portrayal in popular media, Opus Dei primarily focuses on religious teaching and personal holiness.

The **Rosicrucians** are an esoteric organization with roots in early 17th-century Europe, blending elements of mysticism, philosophy, and science. Known for their focus on spiritual enlightenment and the study of the occult, Rosicrucians have influenced Western thought on matters of the soul, nature, and alchemy. Though not overtly secretive today, the Rosicrucian teachings and their symbolism, such as the rose and cross, have contributed to their enigmatic reputation. The Rosicrucians' influence on the arts and sciences and their exploration of hidden knowledge continue to intrigue those interested in spirituality and mysticism.

The **Priory of Sion** gained global attention due to its portrayal in fiction like The DaVinci Code, which alleged its involvement in protecting ancient religious secrets and preserving bloodlines. While historical evidence supporting the Priory's existence is tenuous, its myth continues to captivate imaginations. According to legend, the Priory of Sion was established in medieval Europe, allegedly tied to influential figures and secret relics. Despite the lack of conclusive proof, it symbolizes the public's fascination with the possibility of hidden societies that guard sacred knowledge.

The **Bohemian Club**, founded in 1872 in San Francisco, is an exclusive men's club that annually hosts a retreat at Bohemian Grove in California. Attended by businessmen, artists, and politicians, these gatherings are known for their secrecy and unusual ceremonies, including the famous "Cremation of Care" ritual. Although not a traditional secret society, the club's elite membership and peculiar traditions have spread rumors about its influence on American politics and business. Conspiracy theorists suggest that decisions made at Bohemian Grove shape U.S. policy, though members maintain that the retreat is a social gathering.

Established in 1973, the **Trilateral Commission** is a non-governmental organization that brings together leaders from North America, Europe, and Asia to discuss global issues and foster cooperation. Founded by American banker David Rockefeller, the commission was accused of promoting an international agenda and diminishing national sovereignty. While the Trilateral Commission is relatively open about its goals, critics argue that it represents a concentration of power in the hands of an elite few. Its influence on global economic policy and diplomacy has made it a focus of skepticism among those wary of centralized authority.

The **Hermetic Order of the Golden Dawn** was a British occult society founded in the late 19th century. It was dedicated to studying magic, alchemy, and spiritual development. Influential in Western mysticism, the Golden Dawn attracted poets, writers, and intellectuals, including notable members like W.B. Yeats. While it was highly secretive during its peak, the Golden Dawn's teachings influenced many modern occult practices and inspired the New Age movement. Its complex rituals and dedication to mystical study continue to fascinate occult and esoteric philosophy students.

Each group, from the Freemasons to the Golden Dawn, holds a unique place in history, blending elements of secrecy, exclusivity, and often public intrigue. Though their activities and goals vary, these organizations exemplify the allure of secret societies and the power of mystery. While some groups work towards charitable or philosophical ends, others are accused of wielding hidden influence over world affairs. Regardless of the truth behind these perceptions, secret societies remain symbols of an enigmatic world that straddles the line between myth and reality, ensuring their mystique endures for future generations.

Secret Societies and Everyday People

Though secret societies operate in relative seclusion, their influence sometimes reaches everyday people, subtly or directly.

1. **Cultural Influence:** Symbols and traditions from societies like the Freemasons can be found in architecture, currency, and popular media, influencing how people perceive power and mystery.

2. **Political and Economic Power:** Many believe secret societies influence leadership and decision-making. Elite connections within societies can shape policies, indirectly affecting daily life.

3. **Conspiracy Theories:** People engage with secret societies every day through conspiracy theories. True or false stories shape perceptions of power and influence, sometimes leading to distrust of authority.

4. **Charitable and Social Engagement:** Some societies, such as the Freemasons, contribute positively through charity. Their involvement in community initiatives makes their influence tangible in everyday life.

5. **Shaping Public Thought:** The principles upheld by secret societies, such as Freemasonry's emphasis on integrity and brotherhood, can resonate with broader social values.

6. **Family and Friends:** Every day, people may unknowingly interact with members of secret societies through family, friends, or community leaders who are part of such groups.

Despite their secretive nature, secret societies have a role in shaping public thought, social structures, and cultural norms. Whether through direct actions, cultural influence, or public fascination, these societies impact society by creating a blend of myth, fear, intrigue, and actual influence, reflecting the complex interplay of truth and lies in our world.

Caring about secret societies in relation to truth stems from their potential influence on societal structures, decision-making, and access to information. Here's why secret societies are significant when considering the concept of truth:

Secret societies often include members in influential positions, such as politics, finance, or media. If these groups operate without transparency, their agendas may shape public policies and societal norms in ways that aren't openly disclosed, obscuring the truth about who truly holds power and makes decisions.

Secrecy inherently limits access to information. If a society controls or influences key narratives while concealing its involvement, the public's understanding of events or issues may be distorted. This secrecy hinders informed decision-making and undermines democratic principles.

Secret societies often justify their lack of transparency through the need for discretion or exclusivity. This raises ethical questions about whether the pursuit of their goals aligns with broader societal values. If their actions harm others or perpetuate inequality, they erode trust in systems meant to promote fairness and truth.

Historically, secret societies like the Freemasons, Illuminati, or other clandestine groups have been linked to significant social, political, and economic movements. While some claim they aim for altruistic or philosophical goals, others argue they manipulate events for self-interest. This duality fuels speculation and creates an environment where truth becomes subjective and polarized.

The secretive nature of these groups often leads to the proliferation of conspiracy theories, which can spread misinformation. Distinguishing fact from fiction becomes challenging when concrete evidence about their activities is sparse, further complicating the pursuit of truth.

Transparency is a cornerstone of accountability. Secret societies challenge this by operating outside public scrutiny. Without accountability, it is difficult to verify whether their actions serve the common good or prioritize narrow, self-serving interests.

Awareness of secret societies promotes critical inquiry and skepticism. By questioning their existence and influence, people develop a more discerning approach to truth, focusing on uncovering hidden motives or biases in the information presented to them.

Secret societies matter in relation to truth because their secrecy can obscure the sources and motivations behind significant societal forces. This challenges transparency, fosters mistrust, and complicates the quest for genuine understanding. Caring about their influence helps promote accountability, critical thinking, and a more equitable pursuit of truth.

Secret societies shape our thinking about truth and lies through their inherent secrecy, the influence they may exert on society, and the cultural narratives surrounding their existence. Here are the ways they impact how we perceive and process truth and deception:

The secrecy of these groups creates an aura of mystery, which can distort our perception of truth:

Curiosity and Speculation – People are drawn to what is hidden, leading to curiosity about secret societies. This often results in speculation, myths, and conspiracy theories, which blur the line between fact and fiction.

Suspicion of Hidden Agendas – Their existence fosters a general skepticism about authority and the possibility that hidden forces manipulate societal structures.

Secret societies create a divide between those who believe they hold significant power and those who dismiss their influence as exaggerated or fictional:

Credibility Crisis – This polarization leads to competing narratives, where it becomes difficult to discern the truth from hyperbole or outright lies.

Echo Chambers – Those who believe in secret societies often seek information that confirms their views, while skeptics dismiss all related discussions, perpetuating confirmation biases on both sides.

The perception that secret societies operate behind the scenes fosters distrust in visible systems of governance and authority:

Erosion of Transparency – People may begin to doubt the truthfulness of official narratives, suspecting that secret agendas influence policies, decisions, and events.

Heightened Conspiracy Thinking – This distrust can spill over into unrelated areas, making people more susceptible to believing other lies or half-truths.

The mere possibility of secret societies controlling or influencing societal outcomes reshapes what people consider "truth":

Hidden Truths – The idea that powerful entities conceal the "real truth" leads people to question the authenticity of widely accepted information.

Relativism – In some cases, the existence of secret societies encourages a relativistic view of truth, where individuals believe that all truths are subjective and context-dependent.

Popular culture often depicts secret societies in stories, movies, and books, shaping public attitudes toward secrecy, power, and deception:

Normalization of Deception – These portrayals can make secrecy and manipulation seem like inevitable aspects of power, blurring ethical boundaries around lying.

Romanticizing the Elite – The mystique surrounding secret societies may lead people to admire their exclusivity or see lying as a necessary tool for success.

Secret societies create gaps in shared understanding, which undermines our ability to collectively discern truth:

Conflicting Information – The lack of transparency and verified information about secret societies leads to conflicting accounts, which muddy the waters of public discourse.

Mistrust of Experts – When people suspect secret societies influence experts or institutions, they may dismiss legitimate knowledge, fueling misinformation.

On the flip side, secret societies can prompt people to critically analyze what they are told:

Questioning Narratives – Their secrecy encourages individuals to dig deeper, scrutinizing information for hidden biases or motives.

Heightened Awareness of Manipulation – Understanding how secrecy can shape narratives helps people recognize similar tactics in other contexts.

Secret societies influence our thinking about truth and lies by fostering curiosity, suspicion, and debate. They challenge the idea of a singular truth, encourage skepticism of authority, and often promote both critical inquiry and mistrust. Their enigmatic nature forces us to confront the complexities of deception, power, and hidden influences in shaping societal narratives.

The shaping of our thinking about truth and lies often comes from a mix of formal and informal groups, institutions, and cultural forces. Beyond secret societies, here are a few other groups and organizations that can influence our perspectives:

Major networks, newspapers, and online platforms frame events and narratives, shaping public opinion about what is true. Algorithms and influencers play a significant role in shaping truth by amplifying certain narratives or suppressing others. Movies, TV shows, and books subtly (or overtly) influence cultural ideas about morality, truth, and deception.

Religious teachings often provide foundational beliefs about truth, morality, and deceit. Leaders and structures within faith communities may shape members' understanding of what is right and wrong, as well as how truth is revealed or obscured.

Propaganda, public statements, and policies influence societal perceptions of truth. Political ideologies and party lines often frame issues in ways that prioritize specific "truths" or reinterpret facts.

Schools and universities influence young minds about what is considered knowledge, critical thinking, and ethical behavior. Curriculum choices and teaching philosophies impact students' perceptions of what is factual or biased.

Marketing campaigns craft narratives to sell products, often shaping perceptions of value, identity, and truth. Public relations efforts can sway public perception about a company or industry, sometimes bending or obscuring the truth.

Peer groups, communities, and online forums establish norms and shared beliefs about what is acceptable or true. Popular culture, traditions, and movements reinforce collective ideas of truth and myth. Researchers and scholars influence public understanding of truth through studies, theories, and dissemination of knowledge.

Institutions like think tanks or research organizations often align with specific interests, potentially shaping their conclusions. Advocacy organizations frame issues in ways that align with their missions, influencing public opinion on social, environmental, and political matters.

The framing of a cause or event can highlight certain truths while downplaying others. Algorithms, search engines, and AI shape the availability and visibility of information, subtly steering societal beliefs. Tech companies often control narratives around privacy, ethics, and truth in digital spaces. Family values and upbringing often shape early understandings of honesty, trust, and deception. Close relationships influence personal experiences of truth and lies.

Groups involved in illicit activities often create elaborate networks of deception to operate, influencing narratives around legality and morality. Organizations or individuals promoting certain schools of philosophy (e.g., postmodernism, existentialism) can deeply influence societal views on the nature of truth. Each of these groups operates on a spectrum, sometimes promoting genuine truth and transparency while other times distorting or manipulating facts to align with their goals or beliefs. The interaction between these influences often shapes a complex web of perceptions around truth and lies in society.

References

Anderson, B. (1983). Imagined communities: Reflections on the origin and spread of nationalism. London: Verso.

Bok, S. (1999). Lying: Moral choice in public and private life. New York, NY: Vintage Books.

Chua, A. (2003). World on fire: How exporting free market democracy breeds ethnic hatred and global instability. New York, NY: Doubleday.

Cohen, R. (1997). Global diasporas: An introduction. Seattle, WA: University of Washington Press.

Ekman, P. (2009). Telling lies: Clues to deceit in the marketplace, politics, and marriage (4th ed.). New York, NY: W.W. Norton & Company.

Fukuyama, F. (1992). The end of history and the last man. New York, NY: Free Press.

Giddens, A. (1990). The consequences of modernity. Stanford, CA: Stanford University Press.

Hofstede, G. (2001). Culture's consequences: Comparing values, behaviors, institutions, and organizations across nations (2nd ed.). Thousand Oaks, CA: SAGE Publications.

Levine, T. R. (2014). Truth-default theory (TDT): A theory of human deception and deception detection. Journal of Language and Social Psychology, 33(4), 378–392. https://doi.org/10.1177/0261927X14535916

Mackey, A. (1924). The history of Freemasonry. New York, NY: Gramercy Books.

Moran, T., Abramson, N. R., & Moran, S. V. (2014). Managing cultural differences (9th ed.). New York, NY: Routledge.

Pinker, S. (2011). The better angels of our nature: Why violence has declined. New York, NY: Viking.

Sennett, R. (1998). The corrosion of character: The personal consequences of work in the new capitalism. New York, NY: W.W. Norton & Company.

Vrij, A. (2008). Detecting lies and deceit: Pitfalls and opportunities (2nd ed.). Hoboken, NJ: Wiley.

Wright, L. (1984). Clean and decent: The history of the bathroom and the WC. London: Penguin Books.

Chapter Six:
DIY Fact Checking

Fact-checking is your tool of empowerment in today's world, where misinformation can quickly spread. One of the critical reasons for fact-checking is to prevent the spread of false information. Whether accidental or intentional, misinformation can circulate rapidly, primarily through social media. By verifying information, you ensure that you don't unknowingly share misleading or false content, preserving the integrity of public discourse and assisting others to make decisions based on facts. Fact-checking promotes media literacy. In today's digital world, anyone can publish information online. It's hard to tell reliable sources from unreliable ones. Fact-checking helps evaluate credibility.

Fact-checking encourages critical thinking and promotes questioning sources before accepting claims, which is especially crucial in politics, economics, or science. By verifying facts, you can make more informed choices, such as voting, managing health, and investing, rather than being swayed by incorrect or manipulative information. Fact-checking fosters a sense of responsibility for your personal opinions and beliefs. When you take the time to verify information, you take ownership of the accuracy of your views. This leads to more thoughtful, evidence-based discussions and avoids arguments built on false premises.

Fact-checking protects against scams and fraud. False information isn't limited to social or political contexts; it can lead to financial loss. By fact-checking claims related to investments, products, or services, people can avoid falling victim to fraud. It plays a critical role in supporting democratic processes. Voters need accurate information to hold politicians accountable. Fact-checking political claims helps ensure that decisions are made based on truth rather than misinformation or manipulation, strengthening democratic institutions. Fact-checking encourages personal responsibility. Taking responsibility creates healthier information where truth is valued and upheld.

Fact-Checking Tips

1. Approach Information with Skepticism – Adopt a mindset of curiosity and doubt when encountering new information. Avoid accepting claims at face value.

2. Identify the Source – Check where the information is coming from. Is it a reputable news outlet, a personal blog, or an unknown website? Trusted, well-established sources are more likely to provide accurate information. Always check the credibility of the source. Reliable sources are reputable organizations, academic institutions, or established experts. Beware of sensationalism or bias in reporting.

3. Check Authors' Credentials – Look up the author's background. Are they experts in the field? What is their reputation? Someone with credible experience is more likely to provide reliable information.

4. Cross-Reference with Multiple Sources – Don't rely on a single source. Cross-check the same information with multiple trusted sources to see if they all report similar facts.

5. Consult Primary Sources – Seek the source of the information. If it references a study, report, or event, find that primary document to verify accuracy.

6. Analyze the Date of the Information – Ensure the information is up-to-date. Outdated facts or old data may no longer be accurate or relevant.

7. Evaluate Source Bias – Consider whether the source has a known bias. Is the outlet or author affiliated with a political party, interest group, or organization that could influence the narrative?

8. Understand the Context – Check the full context of the information. A quote or fact taken from context may mislead you into misunderstanding the whole story.

9. Investigate the Claim's Originality – Look at whether the information has been reported elsewhere or if it is an isolated claim. Sources or broader coverage often provide better context.

10. Look for Red Flags – Be wary of sensationalist headlines, emotionally charged language, or claims that seem "too good to be true." These often indicate misinformation or bias.

11. Check for Logical Fallacies – Ensure the argument presented is logical. Watch out for fallacies like ad hominem attacks, false dichotomies, and strawman arguments, which may signal weak or misleading reasoning.

12. Examine Visuals for Authenticity – If images or videos are involved, use tools like reverse image search (e.g., Google Images) to verify if they have been doctored or taken out of context.

13. Use Fact-Checking Websites – Check claims on trusted sites like Snopes, FactCheck.org, PolitiFact, or Full Fact. These sites specialize in investigating dubious claims.

14. Review Scientific Consensus – For scientific claims, consult the consensus of experts in the field. Use reputable scientific organizations, peer-reviewed journals, or authoritative bodies like the CDC, WHO, or NIH.

15. Examine Data Methodology – Review the methodology if statistics or studies are cited. Were the sample sizes large enough? Were the methods rigorous and unbiased?

16. Check Quoted Experts – If experts are quoted, verify their credentials. Ensure they are actual authorities in the relevant field, not outliers or unqualified individuals.

17. Watch Out for Confirmation Bias—Be mindful of your biases. Don't accept information just because it aligns with your pre-existing beliefs. Objectivity is key.

18. Verify URLs and Domain Names—Pay attention to the website URL. Fake news sites often use URLs similar to legitimate sites but with slight changes (e.g., ".co" instead of ".com").

19. Check for Peer-Reviewed Research – If the claim references scientific research, ensure it has been peer-reviewed. Peer-reviewed studies undergo scrutiny by other experts before being published.

20. Follow the Money – Investigate whether the source of the information has a financial interest in promoting a particular narrative. Conflicts of interest can skew the facts.

21. Consult Subject-Matter Experts – Reach out to knowledgeable people about the subject for their insights. This can help verify technical or highly specialized information.

22. Examine the Language Used – Assess whether the language is objective and neutral or emotionally charged and inflammatory. Credible information typically uses factual, neutral language.

23. Analyze Graphs and Data Visualizations – When encountering charts or graphs, check the axes, scales, and sample sizes to ensure they aren't manipulated to mislead or misrepresent data.

24. Check for Retractions or Corrections – If the source has published the information before, check whether any retractions or corrections have been made. Credible outlets often issue corrections when they make mistakes.

25. Examine Personal Biases – Biases can distort our understanding of facts, leading to flawed conclusions and perpetuating misinformation. Biases act as filters, shaping how we perceive, prioritize, or dismiss information based on preconceptions, emotions, or cultural influences. By recognizing these tendencies, we become more aware of how our perspectives are shaped by personal experiences, societal norms, or group affiliations. This self-awareness fosters critical thinking, encourages open-mindedness, and helps us engage with diverse viewpoints. Ultimately, examining biases ensures a fairer evaluation of facts, supports constructive dialogue, and strengthens our ability to make informed, rational decisions in an increasingly complex world.

Fact-checking takes time. Resist the urge to react quickly, especially if the information provokes strong emotions. Taking a moment to verify facts thoroughly is always worth it. Patience is your ally in the battle against misinformation.

To navigate today's complex information landscape, you must ensure that the sources you rely on are credible, accurate, and reliable. Start by verifying facts across multiple trustworthy sources, checking for consistency in data, and identifying any potential biases. Analyzing the credibility of authors, publication dates, and the expertise behind claims can prevent the spread of misinformation. By approaching information critically, you empower yourself to discern fact from opinion and make informed decisions in an age where misinformation can easily cloud the truth.

References

American Press Institute. (n.d.). The importance of fact-checking and verification in journalism. Retrieved from www.americanpressinstitute.org

Caulfield, M. (2017). Web literacy for student fact-checkers. Retrieved from https://webliteracy.pressbooks.com

FactCheck.org. (n.d.). About us: FactCheck.org's mission and approach. Retrieved from https://www.factcheck.org

Lewandowsky, S., Ecker, U. K., & Cook, J. (2017). Beyond misinformation: Understanding and coping with the "post-truth" era. Journal of Applied Research in Memory and Cognition, 6(4), 353–369. https://doi.org/10.1016/j.jarmac. 2017.07.008

Pennycook, G., & Rand, D. G. (2018). The Implied Truth Effect: Attaching warnings to a subset of fake news stories increases the perceived accuracy of stories without warnings. Management Science, 66(11), 4944–4957. https://doi.org/10.1287/mnsc.2019.3478

PolitiFact. (n.d.). Fact-checking tips and tools. Retrieved from https://www.politifact.com

Snopes. (n.d.). About Snopes and our fact-checking methodology. Retrieved from https://www.snopes.com

Wardle, C., & Derakhshan, H. (2017). Information disorder: Toward an interdisciplinary framework for research and policymaking. Council of Europe. Retrieved from https://www.coe.int

World Health Organization (WHO). (2020). Infodemic management: Managing misinformation during health crises. Retrieved from https://www.who.int

Zimdars, M., & McLeod, K. (2020). Fake news: Understanding media and misinformation in the digital age. Cambridge, MA: MIT Press.

Chapter Seven:
Political Situations

The ability to discern truth from falsehood in political situations is not just a skill, but a crucial tool for maintaining the integrity of a democratic society. Politics often deals with decisions that impact entire populations, from laws governing civil liberties to healthcare, education, and national security policies. When falsehoods or distortions are allowed to increase unchecked, they can sway public opinion and lead to decisions based on misinformation, which can have long-lasting and detrimental effects on society. The truth is essential for informed voting. Elections are the cornerstone of a democracy, and for voters to make sound choices, they need accurate information. This is where your critical thinking comes in, empowering you to separate fact from fiction.

Correct information about the candidates, their policies, and the broader implications of their decisions is not just important, but essential. Political figures or parties may misrepresent facts to gain favor or demonize opponents. If citizens cannot differentiate between truth and lies, they may support harmful policies or elect leaders who do not truly represent their interests. This can lead to the erosion of trust in institutions, increasing political polarization and weakening the foundations of a healthy democratic society. The potential harm of misinformation is not a distant threat, but a pressing issue that needs to be addressed urgently.

Decisions based on incorrect information are often made quickly and can have life-or-death consequences. The spread of misinformation can incite fear, hatred, and violence, destabilizing communities, and relationships between nations. False reports about the actions of a foreign government can lead to unnecessary military conflict, while misleading claims about domestic policies can inflame public protests or unrest. Holding political figures accountable is a crucial aspect of governance. When politicians lie or distort facts, the public plays a vital role in demanding transparency and truth. You are not just a passive recipient of information but an active participant in the democratic process.

Without the ability to identify untruths, corruption, abuses of power, and self-serving agendas can flourish unchecked. Democracy relies not just on the institutions of government but on the active participation of an informed and discerning populace. Politicians employ lies and tactics to manipulate public perception, avoid accountability, and discredit opponents. Understanding common strategies used for lying in political debates and explaining how they work is essential for people to grasp truth and untruths better. It's critical to check ourselves and not rely on others to make that decision for us.

The Partial Truth (Omission): Partial truths present only selective facts while omitting key details that would change the overall meaning or context. This tactic allows a politician to mislead without technically lying, as they share only the portions of information that suit their narrative. For instance, a candidate might highlight a rise in job growth while neglecting to mention that many of the jobs are low-wage or part-time. These partial truths are challenging to refute because they contain some accurate information, forcing opponents to dig deeper to expose the omitted context. This makes the claim seem plausible in the short term, even if it misleads the public.

The Straw Man: The Straw Man technique involves misrepresenting or exaggerating an opponent's argument to create an easier target for criticism. By distorting an opponent's stance, a politician can undermine it without addressing the actual issue. For example, a politician might assert that their opponent wants to "defund the entire military" when the opponent merely supports selective cuts. This tactic diverts attention from the core issues, forcing the opponent to counter an exaggerated claim instead of presenting their actual position, thus shifting the debate in favor of the accuser.

The Bold-Faced Lie: A bold-faced lie involves confidently making an entirely false statement, relying on the idea that people may believe a lie if it's delivered assertively or aligns with their preexisting beliefs. For example, a politician might claim their administration significantly reduced crime rates, even if crime has increased. Bold-faced lies are impactful because they make an immediate impression, often going unchecked by listeners who don't fact-check in real time. This tactic plays on the audience's trust, allowing the lie to gain traction before it can be disproven.

Deflection and Blame Shifting: Instead of addressing a controversial issue or their wrongdoing, a politician may deflect by accusing their opponent of a worse or unrelated offense. For instance, if accused of corruption, a politician might shift focus by bringing up a past scandal involving their opponent, whether relevant or exaggerated. Deflection distracts the audience and prevents direct confrontation, making it harder for viewers to focus on the politician's actions. This tactic keeps the original issue unresolved while casting doubt on the opponent.

Appeal to Emotion: The appeal to emotion tactic leverages strong emotions, such as fear, anger, or patriotism, to distract from factual analysis. A politician can manipulate the audience's perception by evoking powerful feelings, making them more likely to accept a lie without scrutiny. For example, a politician might exaggerate a threat from an external country or group to garner support for a particular policy. Emotional appeals cloud rational judgment, steering focus away from the truth and creating a persuasive narrative that bypasses logical critique.

The Gish Gallop: The Gish Gallop involves overwhelming opponents and the audience with a rapid succession of lies, half-truths, and misleading statements. This barrage of information leaves little time for fact-checking each point, allowing many claims to go unchallenged. For instance, a politician might rattle off a long list of supposed accomplishments, mixing truth with exaggeration. Opponents can address only a few points, leaving the rest unrefuted. This tactic makes the speaker appear well-informed, creating an impression of credibility despite the inaccuracies.

Cherry-Picking Data: Cherry-picking data involves presenting only statistics or facts that support one's argument while ignoring contradictory data. By selectively sharing information, a politician can paint a misleading picture that appears truthful. For instance, a politician might cite GDP growth as a sign of economic success while omitting high unemployment rates or income inequality. This tactic creates an appearance of expertise but only provides part of the story. Opponents must work harder to reveal a balanced perspective, often after the initial message has already made its impact.

Deny and Double Down: When confronted with a lie, some politicians deny it outright and double down, repeating the false claim despite evidence to the contrary. For example, a politician might insist an election was "stolen" even after multiple investigations affirm its legitimacy. This strategy creates confusion and relies on the idea that repeating a lie enough times can make it seem credible to specific audiences. Repetition can reinforce the falsehood, making it appear more believable to those who initially supported the claim.

Ambiguity and Vague Language: Using vague or ambiguous language allows a politician to mislead without committing to a direct lie. By crafting statements that can be interpreted in multiple ways, they can avoid accountability if challenged. For example, saying, "I support reducing taxes for everyone," without specifying that the plan favors the wealthy, creates a misleading impression of fairness. This tactic enables politicians to appeal broadly without clarity, making it difficult for opponents to counter the misleading implications effectively.

Appeal to Authority or False Experts: Citing biased or fake experts and studies lends an air of credibility to a false claim. By invoking authority, a politician can make a statement appear legitimate even if the sources are questionable. For example, quoting a "study" from an unreliable source to support a dubious stance misleads the audience, especially those who lack the time or resources to verify the source. This tactic exploits trust in authority, allowing the lie to gain credibility through association with supposed expertise.

Risks of Lying in Political Debates

Lying during political debates carries substantial risks. While a well-delivered lie might sway public opinion, the fast-paced environment can make it challenging for opponents and fact-checkers to expose falsehoods immediately. However, if the lie is eventually uncovered, it can severely damage the politician's credibility and erode trust among voters. Skilled orators might manage to convince supporters through confidence and persuasive delivery, but these gains are often temporary, as post-debate analysis or media scrutiny can reveal inconsistencies, leading to long-lasting reputational harm. Ultimately, the gamble of lying in a debate poses a high risk of public backlash and diminished career prospects.

Consequences of Lying in a Political Debate

Lying in a political debate can have far-reaching effects, impacting the politician directly and influencing public trust, political dynamics, and democratic institutions.

1. **Loss of Public Trust:** If a politician is caught lying during a debate, public trust can suffer significant damage. Once voters feel deceived, they may lose faith in the politician's ability to govern with integrity, leading to decreased support, lower enthusiasm at the polls, and even broader disillusionment with politics. Loss of trust can harm re- election prospects and perpetuate public cynicism toward political leaders.

2. **Damage to Credibility:** Credibility is invaluable for any politician. A reputation for honesty strengthens a leader's ability to gain support, influence policy, and maintain relationships with colleagues and constituents. When a lie is exposed, however, every future statement may be viewed with suspicion, hindering their ability to lead effectively, and reducing their authority in their party and among the public.

3. **Media Scrutiny and Fact-Checking:** With modern technology, lies told during debates are frequently and quickly analyzed by the media and fact-checkers, often resulting in rapid debunking. This scrutiny can dominate the post-debate coverage, diverting attention from a politician's intended messages. If a lie becomes the focal point of media discussions, it can overshadow any achievements or positive aspects of their campaign, intensifying the damage to their public image.

4. **Reputational Damage:** Lies told in debates can lead to long-term reputational damage, as opponents and critics will likely highlight dishonesty in future campaigns, debates, and advertisements. A politician known for lying may struggle to regain credibility, making it harder to advance in their career. Once a reputation for dishonesty takes hold, it can become an enduring obstacle in any political ambitions.

5. **Voter Backlash:** When voters discover that a politician lied, especially about core campaign promises or positions, they may feel deeply betrayed. This backlash can manifest as lower voter turnout, increased protest, or a shift in support to an opponent. Losing voter trust impacts the individual politician and can weaken support for their entire party if the lie is tied to broader party ideologies or policies.

6. **Legal and Ethical Consequences:** Some lies in political debates, particularly those involving national security, public policy, or election integrity, can lead to legal and ethical repercussions. If a politician lies about sensitive matters, it may trigger investigations or legal actions, including congressional scrutiny or impeachment proceedings, depending on the issue's gravity.

7. **Polarization and Divisiveness:** Lies that exploit emotional or divisive issues can deepen societal rifts. Misleading claims about contentious topics like immigration, race, or national security can stoke anger and prejudice, making political discourse more polarized. This divisiveness complicates the government's ability to address critical issues and increases gridlock.

8. **Undermining Democratic Institutions:** Lies about fundamental democratic processes, such as election integrity, can erode trust in these institutions, weakening public faith in the electoral system, judiciary, and media. When citizens lose confidence in these pillars of democracy, the stability of democratic governance is compromised, opening the door to authoritarian influence, and weakening public trust.

9. **Decreased International Credibility:** Lies from high-ranking officials can damage a nation's reputation on the world stage. International leaders may become wary of diplomatic engagements with dishonest politicians, hindering collaboration on global issues. The loss of credibility abroad can weaken a nation's influence and diminish its ability to negotiate effectively in trade, defense, and other vital areas.

10. **Empowerment of Opponents:** A lie in a debate allows opponents to discredit the politician. Opponents can portray the liar as dishonest or untrustworthy, weakening their standing with undecided voters. The lie can shift momentum in the race, mainly if it involves critical issues voters care about, and serve as a focal point in campaign strategies against the politician.

11. **Reinforcement of Echo Chambers:** If a politician lies and then doubles down, this tactic can reinforce echo chambers among loyal supporters who may accept the lie as fact, isolating them from

differing views. These echo chambers hinder constructive dialogue by reinforcing partisan divides and limiting supporters' ability to engage with opposing perspectives.

12. **Potential Personal and Family Impact:** In some cases, politicians' personal lives may suffer due to public lies. Family members might face public scrutiny, harassment, or even threats, adding stress and embarrassment to their lives. Media attention on a lie can amplify these personal challenges, creating lasting social and emotional consequences for politicians and their loved ones.

Lying in political debates can yield serious, often irreversible consequences, from harming a politician's career to undermining public faith in democratic systems. In today's age of widespread media coverage and real-time fact-checking, the risks of lying often outweigh the temporary gains, emphasizing the importance of honesty in political discourse.

The consequences of lying in a political debate go far beyond the moment, making it essential for people to understand and assess the truth. Political debates are critical forums where candidates present their policies, values, and visions, influencing how voters make decisions. When candidates lie, they distort this process, misleading the public about their qualifications, intentions, or the viability of their proposals.

Assessing the truth allows individuals to make informed choices. Lies in debates can lead to poorly crafted policies, such as ineffective healthcare reforms, misguided economic strategies, or inadequate climate action. These can have real-world consequences, affecting jobs, health, and the environment for years. By seeking the truth, individuals can better understand which policies align with reality and will benefit society.

Moreover, lies in debates erode trust in political systems. Democracies rely on a belief that leaders are truthful and act in the public's best interest. Exposing dishonesty fosters accountability and prevents a culture of deception from taking root. When individuals actively assess the truth, they contribute to maintaining this trust and upholding the integrity of the democratic process.

Critically evaluating the truth also helps combat polarization. Lies often fuel divisions, creating echo chambers where people cling to false narratives. By prioritizing facts, individuals can engage in more productive, evidence-based discussions. In holding candidates accountable for truthfulness, individuals not only safeguard democracy but also empower themselves to demand leaders who act with integrity and prioritize the common good.

Following are twelve examples of political lies and their consequences:

Donald Trump (U.S. President) In 2020, Trump downplayed the severity of COVID-19 publicly, despite acknowledging its dangers in private conversations with journalist Bob Woodward. Trump's depreciation of the pandemic's threat led many to underestimate the virus, affecting public health responses and contributing to widespread confusion and polarization. The revelation eroded trust in his handling of the pandemic, with critics accusing him of placing political image over public safety. This incident underscored how misinformation on health issues can profoundly affect public trust and lives.

Boris Johnson (UK Prime Minister) Johnson's claim during the 2019 Brexit campaign that £350 million per week would be redirected to the National Health Service (NHS) after leaving the EU was widely criticized as misleading. The figure, later debunked, fueled public support for Brexit but ultimately damaged Johnson's credibility. Once the inaccuracy was revealed, many felt manipulated, and trust in Johnson's leadership suffered, with critics accusing him of exploiting misinformation for political gain. This episode demonstrated how financial falsehoods can sway national decisions and alter public trust.

The SNC-Lavalin scandal involving Canadian Prime Minister Justin Trudeau began in 2019. Initially, Trudeau denied interfering in a criminal case involving SNC-Lavalin, an engineering firm accused of corruption. However, testimony from then-Attorney General Jody Wilson-Raybould revealed that Trudeau and his office had pressured her to consider an alternative to prosecution for the firm, such as a deferred prosecution agreement. This contradicted Trudeau's public statements, sparking accusations of unethical behavior and abuse of power. The scandal significantly damaged Trudeau's image as a leader committed to transparency and ethics, creating public disillusionment, and straining his political support. Trudeau's actions stained his image as a champion of transparency and integrity, causing disillusionment among supporters. The scandal highlighted how ethical lapses and dishonesty in political leadership can undermine trust and lead to significant public backlash.

Sarah Huckabee Sanders (White House Press Secretary) In 2017, Sanders falsely claimed that "countless" FBI agents had lost confidence in Director James Comey, whom President Trump had fired. Sanders later admitted the statement was untrue, damaging her credibility and reinforcing skepticism about the administration's transparency. The lie, which influenced public perception of Comey's dismissal, underscored the risks of providing misinformation, especially when representing the executive branch. It highlighted how mistrust can develop when official spokespersons are caught manipulating facts. Despite the controversy, Sanders went on to rebuild her political career and later became the Governor of Arkansas, further cementing her role in U.S. politics.

Mitt Romney (U.S. Senator) During his 2012 presidential campaign, Romney falsely claimed that Jeep was moving jobs from the U.S. to China, which Jeep promptly refuted. Romney's statement was seen as fearmongering aiming to sway voters in crucial swing states. The backlash damaged Romney's credibility on economic issues, with critics accusing him of using misleading information to gain support. This incident demonstrated how economic falsehoods can backfire, hurting a candidate's reputation and credibility with the voters they aim to persuade.

Hillary Clinton (U.S. Secretary of State) After the 2012 attack on the U.S. consulate in Benghazi, Secretary of State Hillary Clinton initially attributed the violence to a protest over a video, despite later findings that it was a coordinated terrorist attack. Her statements drew intense scrutiny and accusations of misleading the public about the events leading to the deaths of four Americans. This perceived lack of transparency damaged Clinton's reputation, especially among those questioning her integrity and decision-making. The incident became a focal point for critics, highlighting how discrepancies in recounting sensitive events can affect public perception of leaders.

Paul Ryan (U.S. Congressman) inaccurately claimed to have run a marathon in under three hours during an interview in 2012. He made the statement on a radio show hosted by Hugh Hewitt, where he said he had run a marathon in "two hours and fifty-something." However, it was later revealed that his actual time in the 1990 Grandma's Marathon in Duluth, Minnesota, was 4 hours, 1 minute, and 25 seconds. Ryan admitted to the inaccuracy, attributing it to a misremembering of his time. While seemingly trivial, the exaggeration led to public criticism, as it reflected on

Ryan's personal integrity and honesty. Though minor compared to other political lies, this incident illustrated how even small falsehoods can undermine trust and create unnecessary distractions, leading to questions about a politician's credibility in personal and professional matters.

Anthony Weiner (U.S. Congressman) In 2011, Weiner initially denied sending explicit photos via Twitter, claiming his account was hacked. When evidence revealed that he had sent the pictures, he admitted to his actions, leading to his resignation. Weiner's dishonesty damaged his political career and cast doubt on his character, leading to public embarrassment and loss of credibility. This scandal emphasized how personal misconduct, when covered up, can lead to career-ending consequences and a public reputation that may never recover.

George W. Bush (U.S. President) In 2003, President George W. Bush's claim that Iraq possessed weapons of mass destruction (WMDs) served as a primary justification for the Iraq invasion. When no WMDs were found, public trust in Bush's administration suffered, with many Americans feeling misled into supporting a costly war. This false claim had long-term consequences, including loss of life, destabilization in the Middle East, and diminished U.S. credibility globally. Bush's decision has been criticized as one of the most significant intelligence failures, emphasizing the risks of misrepresentation in national security matters.

Tony Blair (UK Prime Minister) British Prime Minister Blair's support for the Iraq War in 2003 relied heavily on the assertion that Iraq had WMDs, aligning with George W. Bush's stance. Blair's reputation was tarnished when the Chilcot Report revealed unreliable intelligence supporting this claim. The revelation led to widespread public disillusionment in the UK, with many questioning Blair's judgment and motivations. Blair's involvement in this misinformation campaign contributed to a broader distrust of political leaders and highlighted the consequences of aligning with controversial international policies based on faulty evidence.

Bill Clinton (U.S. President) In 1998, President Bill Clinton's denial of an affair with White House intern Monica Lewinsky led to an impeachment scandal after he was found to have lied under oath. Initially stating he had "not had sexual relations with that woman," Clinton's admission of the affair contradicted his earlier public statements, sparking a divisive trial in the Senate. Clinton's lie damaged his credibility and overshadowed his administration's achievements. The scandal fostered a contentious political climate and reinforced concerns about personal integrity and truthfulness among public officials.

The idea that the Bill Clinton-Monica Lewinsky affair distracted national attention and contributed to the events leading up to the World Trade Center bombing in 1993 and the 9/11 attacks is a perspective that combines political and historical analysis. Here's how the connection can be drawn:

The Clinton-Lewinsky scandal, which dominated headlines in the late 1990s, shifted much of the government and media's focus toward internal political drama rather than external threats. The scandal consumed substantial time and resources as Congress debated impeachment, and the public and policymakers were preoccupied with sensational coverage. Some argue this distraction may have reduced attention to growing international threats, such as Al-Qaeda.

During this period, Al-Qaeda was actively planning and conducting attacks, including the 1998 U.S. embassy bombings in Kenya and Tanzania. Critics argue that the administration's ability to respond comprehensively to these threats was hampered by the focus on domestic scandals. While counterterrorism efforts continued, some believe they lacked the urgency or coordination required to disrupt plots in their early stages.

By the late 1990s, Osama bin Laden had been identified as a key threat to U.S. security. The Clinton administration attempted to kill or capture him multiple times, but these efforts were constrained by various factors, including limited political will and international challenges. Critics suggest that the distraction of the scandal weakened the administration's ability to prioritize and act decisively on such threats.

The political turmoil of the Lewinsky scandal contributed to a fragmented domestic political environment, potentially limiting the administration's ability to lay the groundwork for a more robust, bipartisan counterterrorism strategy. This may have left gaps that were not adequately addressed before the 9/11 attacks.

It's important to note that terrorism is a complex phenomenon influenced by numerous global factors, including geopolitical dynamics, regional instability, and ideological movements. The Clinton-Lewinsky affair was one of many elements shaping U.S. policy and focus during that period. Al-Qaeda's development as a threat spanned multiple administrations, and systemic issues, such as intelligence sharing and national security priorities, also played significant roles.

While the Clinton-Lewinsky affair undeniably shifted attention and resources during a critical period, it is overly simplistic to assign direct causation between the scandal and the 1993 World Trade Center bombing or 9/11. These events were the culmination of years of planning and broader geopolitical developments. Examining how political distractions impact national security decisions highlights the importance of maintaining focus on external threats, even amid domestic crises.

Richard Nixon (U.S. President) In 1972, President Richard Nixon's denial of involvement in the Watergate scandal ultimately led to a profound crisis of trust in the American government. His attempts to cover up the break-in at the Democratic National Committee headquarters were revealed through the infamous "Watergate tapes," exposing him as complicit in obstructing justice. The scandal became one of the most significant political betrayals in U.S. history, leading to Nixon's resignation in 1974 to avoid impeachment. This event underscored the consequences of political deceit at the highest level, fueling widespread cynicism toward politicians and casting a long-lasting shadow over the American presidency.

These examples reveal that lies in politics, regardless of their scope, can have profound and often irreversible repercussions. When political leaders deceive the public, trust can be eroded in the individual and the entire institution they represent, creating a ripple effect that weakens the foundation of democratic systems. Lies that go unchallenged can lead to public disillusionment, where citizens may become apathetic or distrustful of all political figures, viewing dishonesty as a norm rather than an exception. This erosion of trust makes it harder for future leaders to earn public confidence, potentially resulting in decreased voter turnout, heightened political cynicism, and an increasingly polarized society.

The consequences extend beyond national borders, as lies such as war, international diplomacy, and global health undermine a nation's credibility on the world stage. Foreign allies may become reluctant to collaborate, and adversaries may exploit perceived weaknesses, leading to strained diplomatic relationships and diminished influence in international organizations. For the individuals involved, being caught in a lie can lead to career setbacks, loss of public support, and even legal ramifications, as political opponents and the media hold them accountable. Moreover, political lies can create dangerous precedents, encouraging future leaders to stretch the truth for short-term gain, further deepening the cycle of mistrust. Ultimately, these incidents underscore how essential honesty and transparency are in maintaining the integrity of governance and fostering a stable, trustworthy relationship between leaders and the people they serve.

References

Bok, S. (1999). Lying: Moral choice in public and private life. New York, NY: Vintage Books.

Cook, J., & Lewandowsky, S. (2011). The debunking handbook. University of Queensland. Retrieved from https://skepticalscience.com

FactCheck.org. (n.d.). Holding politicians accountable through fact-checking. Retrieved from https://www.factcheck.org

Flynn, D. J., Nyhan, B., & Reifler, J. (2017). The nature and origins of misperceptions: Understanding false and unsupported beliefs about politics. Political Psychology, 38(S1), 127–150. https://doi.org/10.1111/pops.12394

Hofstadter, R. (1964). The paranoid style in American politics. New York, NY: Knopf.

Jamieson, K. H., & Capella, J. N. (2008). Echo chamber: Rush Limbaugh and the conservative media establishment. New York, NY: Oxford University Press.

Lewandowsky, S., Ecker, U. K. H., & Cook, J. (2017). Beyond misinformation: Understanding and coping with the "post-truth" era. Journal of Applied Research in Memory and Cognition, 6(4), 353–369. https://doi.org/10.1016/j.jarmac.2017.07.008

PolitiFact. (n.d.). Tracking political lies and their consequences. Retrieved from https://www.politifact.com

Snopes. (n.d.). Verifying claims in political discourse. Retrieved from https://www.snopes.com

Wardle, C., & Derakhshan, H. (2017). Information disorder: Toward an interdisciplinary framework for research and policymaking. Council of Europe. Retrieved from https://www.coe.int

Zaller, J. R. (1992). The nature and origins of mass opinion. New York, NY: Cambridge University Press.

Chapter Eight:
Social Situations

D iscerning the truth from untruth in social situations is crucial for building and maintaining community trust. On a personal level, honesty fosters more robust relationships among friends, family, or colleagues. When untruths are introduced through gossip, manipulation, or misunderstanding, it can erode trust, lead to conflict, and cause emotional harm. This principle holds even greater significance on a broader societal level, as social cohesion depends on shared understandings of reality.

Addressing the issue of misinformation spread by well-intentioned individuals is crucial in a world where false information can travel quickly and have significant consequences. People often share misinformation, believing it to be true, a phenomenon fueled by cognitive biases, social echo chambers, and the sheer volume of information online. This unintentional spread of falsehoods can erode trust, distort public discourse, and influence critical decisions on matters like health, politics, and social policy.

When individuals share misinformation, it can amplify misunderstandings, polarize communities, and create resistance to corrective facts. For instance, misinformation about vaccines has led to decreased immunization rates, compromising public health. Similarly, sharing inaccurate political information can undermine democratic processes, leading to flawed decision-making and diminished trust in institutions.

To address this issue, fostering media literacy and critical thinking is vital. Encouraging individuals to question sources, verify facts, and avoid impulsive sharing can significantly reduce the spread of misinformation. Social media platforms also have a role in flagging or limiting the reach of unverified content. Fact-checking organizations can provide clear, accessible corrections to widely spread inaccuracies.

Acknowledging the psychological reasons behind this behavior, such as confirmation bias and emotional resonance, is also key. Compassionate education, rather than punitive responses, helps create an environment where individuals feel empowered to question and revise their beliefs.

Ultimately, addressing this challenge strengthens societal resilience against misinformation, ensuring decisions and discussions are grounded in truth, thereby fostering trust and cohesion in a rapidly evolving information landscape.

Social media, where much of modern social interaction occurs, has become a breeding ground for misinformation. People often share news stories, opinions, and rumors without verifying accuracy. This can lead to the rapid spread of false narratives, distorting public perceptions and sow division. In extreme cases, these falsehoods can lead to real-world consequences, such as the harassment of innocent individuals, the spread of dangerous medical misinformation, or the reinforcement of harmful stereotypes.

In professional or organizational settings, the ability to discern truth from lies is essential for teamwork and productivity. When colleagues or leaders are not truthful, it can create a toxic environment where trust diminishes and communication breaks down. Leaders who misrepresent information may exploit their position, taking advantage of those who cannot distinguish between true and false. Employees or team members who propagate untruths can sabotage efforts, leading to poor decision-making, wasted resources, and a lack of accountability.

Spotting untruths helps combat prejudice and discrimination on a societal level. Many social issues, such as racism, sexism, and xenophobia, are perpetuated by false beliefs or exaggerated narratives about certain groups of people. These untruths can become ingrained in the collective consciousness, fueling hatred and systemic inequalities. Individuals can contribute to a more just and equitable society by recognizing and challenging these falsehoods.

In social contexts, lying is often a quick fix to avoid conflict, preserve social standing, or spare someone's feelings. These lies can have lasting repercussions, from damaging trust to later creating conflict.

People employ several common strategies when lying in social situations, including motivations and potential consequences.

1. **White Lies** - People often tell small, seemingly harmless lies, known as "white lies," to avoid awkwardness or spare someone's feelings. For instance, saying, "I love your new haircut," even when it's not true, can be a way to make someone feel good and maintain social harmony. These lies smooth over minor discomforts and help

navigate sensitive situations where honesty might feel unnecessarily harsh.

The acceptability of white lies depends on context and intent. While they can foster goodwill in the short term, they may lead to unintended consequences if discovered. For example, the person might feel foolish or betrayed, even though the intention was kind. This can create distrust in future interactions, undermining relationships over time.

Frequent reliance on white lies can blur the lines between small deceptions and more significant dishonesty, making it harder to discern when truth is necessary. Honesty, when delivered with empathy, often strengthens connections, and builds trust, even in challenging situations. The acceptability of white lies hinges on whether they serve to protect someone's feelings without causing harm or if they risk eroding trust. Striking a balance between kindness and truthfulness is key—choosing words that are both honest and considerate can often achieve the same purpose without resorting to deception.

2. **Exaggeration** involves embellishing the truth to create a favorable impression or win admiration. For example, someone might claim they received a promotion at work when they're just in consideration for it. Exaggeration can make social interactions more engaging and boost one's image temporarily. However, if others discover the truth, it can harm the exaggerator's credibility, leading to embarrassment and potentially making others question their honesty in all situations.

3. **Lying by Omission** is when someone leaves out key details to create a misleading impression. This tactic allows the person to avoid a direct lie while controlling the narrative. For example, a person might tell a friend that a work presentation went well but fail to mention they arrived late. People use omissions to evade criticism or maintain a positive image without lying outright. Once others discover omitted details, it can cause feelings of manipulation and disappointment, leading to distrust.

4. **Deflection** involves redirecting attention away from an uncomfortable truth by changing the subject. For instance, when

asked if they completed a task, a person might respond with, "Did you hear about the new project?" Deflection is a tactic for avoiding immediate confrontation and uncomfortable conversations. While it works in the short term, frequent deflection can lead people to view the deflector as evasive and unreliable, potentially straining relationships over time.

5. **Blaming Someone Else** - Shifting blame allows someone to avoid responsibility for a mistake by placing it on someone else. For example, employees might tell their boss, "I couldn't finish the report because so-and-so didn't send me the numbers," when they didn't follow up. People use this tactic to protect their image and avoid repercussions, but it often leads to resentment from others. If exposed, the liar appears cowardly, damaging relationships and losing respect among colleagues or friends.

6. **Fabrication** involves creating entirely false stories or details to deceive others. Someone might claim they've traveled extensively to impress others when they haven't. People fabricate to enhance their social status or make themselves seem more attractive. However, fabricated lies are especially risky since they can often be disproven. Once exposed, fabricators can face severe reputational damage, with others viewing them as untrustworthy or inauthentic.

7. **The "Good Intention" Lie** is justified as being in the recipient's best interest, often to protect their feelings. For example, a person might say, "You did great at your presentation," even if it went poorly, to avoid discouraging them. Though these lies stem from kindness, if the person later discovers the truth, they may feel embarrassed or hurt, feeling that others weren't honest enough to offer genuine feedback.

The impact of lying in social settings varies depending on the context, the lie's significance, and the relationship between the people involved. Here are some potential outcomes:

1. **Loss of Trust** is fundamental to social relationships. When someone is caught lying, even about minor matters, it can erode trust and create suspicion in future interactions. Broken trust is hard to rebuild, and

friends or colleagues may become wary of the liar's intentions, casting doubt on their honesty in other areas.

2. **Damaged Relationships** - Lies, especially those affecting significant matters, can harm relationships on a deep emotional level. When dishonesty is discovered, it can lead to resentment, hurt, or even the end of the relationship. Friends, family, or partners who feel betrayed may struggle to reconcile with the liar, leading to permanent fractures in the relationship.

3. **Reputation Damage** - Being labeled a liar can harm a person's reputation within their social group or community. Once caught in a lie, word spreads, leading others to see the individual as untrustworthy. This can result in social isolation, loss of respect, and difficulty forming new relationships, as others may be wary of associating with someone perceived as dishonest.

4. **Increased Stress and Anxiety** - Keeping track of lies can be mentally and emotionally exhausting. The fear of being exposed, the pressure of remembering the details, and the need for further deception to cover up original lies can lead to significant anxiety. Chronic liars may experience heightened stress and guilt, potentially impacting their overall mental health and well-being.

5. **Escalation of Lies (Snowball Effect)** - One lie often leads to another, as the liar tries to maintain the falsehood or cover up its exposure. This escalation creates a complex web of deceit that becomes harder to manage. The more elaborate the lies, the greater the risk of being caught, leading to more severe fallout if the deception unravels.

6. **Loss of Opportunities** - Lying in professional or social settings can limit future opportunities, as people may view the liar as unreliable or untrustworthy. This can mean missed promotions, strained relationships with colleagues, or job loss in the workplace. Socially, it might result in fewer invitations to gatherings or group activities.

7. **Emotional Harm to Others** - Even well-intentioned lies can hurt others, especially if they discover the truth later. Lies meant to protect feelings can have the opposite effect, causing more profound

emotional pain once the person realizes they were misled. This can lead to lingering feelings of anger or sadness, damaging relationships.

8. **Social Isolation** - Frequent lying can lead others to avoid the liar, as they may not want to engage with someone they can't trust. This isolation can decrease social interactions, leaving the liar feeling excluded or marginalized from their social circle, which can have lasting effects on their social life and sense of belonging.

While lying in social situations may temporarily escape awkwardness or conflict, the long-term consequences often outweigh any short-term benefits. Lying erodes trust, damages reputations, and can lead to increased stress, social isolation, and damaged relationships. Trust is difficult to regain once lost, and the ripple effects of lying can extend through both personal and professional aspects of life.

Lying in an economic context typically involves presenting false information to gain financial advantages, protect assets, or manipulate markets. These lies can occur in various settings, including corporate boardrooms, financial markets, or government economic policy.

Below are common strategies used for lying in economic situations:

Falsifying Financial Statements - Companies or individuals may intentionally alter financial records to misrepresent their economic health. This could involve inflating profits, understating losses, or hiding liabilities to present a stronger financial position than reality. As an example, Enron famously falsified financial statements by using complex accounting tricks to hide debts and inflate profits. The goal is often to maintain or increase investor confidence, secure loans, or avoid regulatory scrutiny. Companies may also want to increase their stock price or executive bonuses based on "improved" performance. While it can provide short-term benefits, if discovered, it can lead to legal action, loss of investor trust, and the company's collapse.

Insider Trading occurs when someone with privileged, non-public information about a company's financial future lies or withholds that information to profit from trading its stock or securities. Martha Stewart was convicted of lying about her insider trading activities when she sold stock based on non-public information. The primary motivation is personal financial gain. By acting on information before it becomes public, traders can buy or sell shares to maximize profits or minimize losses. Insider trading is illegal and carries significant legal consequences, including fines, imprisonment, and reputational damage.

Ponzi Schemes occur when the scammer lies about the source of returns, promising high, consistent returns to new investors while using money from later investors to pay earlier ones. There is no legitimate business activity generating profits. Bernie Madoff ran one of the most infamous Ponzi schemes in history, promising investors consistent returns while using new investments to pay off earlier investors. Ponzi schemes allow scammers to accumulate large sums of money quickly by deceiving investors with promises of easy, consistent profits. Ponzi schemes are unsustainable and collapse when new investments dry up, leading to massive financial losses for investors. Perpetrators face criminal charges, imprisonment, and the destruction of their reputations.

Misleading Advertising or Fraudulent Marketing occurs when businesses misrepresent the benefits or features of a product or service to boost sales. This could involve overstating a product's effectiveness, safety, or returns on investment. Volkswagen was caught lying about emissions levels in their "clean diesel" vehicles to deceive consumers and regulators. The aim of misleading advertising or fraudulent marketing is to increase revenue, market share, or stock value by enticing customers to purchase under pretenses. Exposing the truth can lead to lawsuits, government fines, loss of customer trust, and brand damage.

Tax Evasion is evidenced when lying about income, expenses, or other financial details on tax returns reduce the amount of taxes owed. This can involve underreporting income, inflating deductions, or hiding assets in offshore accounts. The Panama Papers revealed that numerous high-profile individuals and companies were caught engaging in tax evasion, including the use of offshore tax havens. The goal of tax evasion is to pay less in taxes, retain more earnings, and avoid government scrutiny. Tax evasion can lead to criminal charges, heavy fines, and even imprisonment. Additionally, being caught can result in reputational damage and an increased likelihood of future audits.

Price Fixing and Collusion - Companies may secretly agree to set prices at artificially high levels rather than competing in a free market. This involves lying to regulators or customers about the nature of the competitive environment. The major automotive parts suppliers colluded to fix prices, leading to a global investigation and fines. Price fixing allows companies to avoid price wars and increase profits at the expense of consumers. Price- fixing is illegal in most countries. If discovered, companies and executives face steep fines, legal actions, and loss of public trust.

Stock Market Manipulation involves spreading false or misleading information about a company or security to drive the stock price up or down for personal gain. This can occur through false rumors, "pump and dump" schemes, or manipulating trading volumes. Jordan Belfort, the "Wolf of Wall Street," was convicted of stock manipulation, defrauding investors in various penny stock schemes. Personal or corporate financial gain is the primary goal. Manipulators often aim to sell at inflated prices or buy artificially low ones. Market manipulation is illegal, and those caught face criminal charges, fines, and imprisonment. It also erodes public confidence in the financial markets.

Corporate Espionage and Misappropriation of Trade Secrets occurs when companies or individuals lie to obtain competitors' trade secrets or sensitive financial information. This can involve corporate espionage, bribery, or other deceptive tactics. High-profile corporate espionage cases include companies stealing proprietary technologies or trade secrets to gain an edge in the market. The objective is to gain a competitive advantage without investing in research and development or to use confidential information to undercut rivals. Corporate espionage is illegal, and those involved face severe legal consequences, including financial penalties and imprisonment. It can also result in damaged reputations and loss of business.

Manipulating Economic Data occurs when governments or financial institutions lie or manipulate economic data such as inflation rates, unemployment figures, or GDP growth to create a false sense of stability or prosperity. Greece was accused of manipulating its budget deficit figures during the lead-up to the European debt crisis, which contributed to its financial collapse in 2010. The purpose is often to maintain investor confidence, attract foreign investment, or win elections by presenting a false picture of economic health. When the truth is uncovered, it can lead to economic crises, loss of investor trust, severe financial repercussions for the country involved, and political upheaval.

Loan Fraud involves lying on loan applications to secure financing. This can involve falsifying income, employment status, or other details to obtain a loan for which the individual or company may not qualify. During the 2008 financial crisis, many lenders accepted mortgage applications with minimal scrutiny, often overlooking inaccuracies or exaggerated claims from homebuyers. While some homebuyers may not have intentionally misrepresented their information, lenders were willing to approve loans with little regard for verification, contributing to the housing market collapse. The goal is to obtain funds that the individual or business would not otherwise be eligible for, often to invest, expand operations, or make large purchases. If the fraud is exposed, the borrower faces legal consequences, including fines and potential jail time. Additionally, the loan is likely to be called in, leading to financial difficulties or bankruptcy.

Misrepresenting Investment Risks - Financial advisors or institutions may lie about the risks of certain investments to sell more products or attract more investors. This could involve downplaying the dangers of high-risk ventures like hedge funds, startups, or volatile markets. The 2008 financial crisis was partly fueled by financial institutions lying about the risks associated with mortgage-backed securities. The goal is to make investments seem safer or more profitable than they are, attracting more investors and increasing commissions or profits. Misrepresenting risks can lead to massive financial losses for investors, lawsuits, regulatory action, and reputational damage for the institutions involved.

False Promises to Employees is when companies lie to employees about the stability of the business, upcoming promotions, or compensation changes to retain staff or avoid mass resignations. Some companies promise bonuses or raises that never materialize to keep employees motivated during difficult times. The goal is to keep employees productive and loyal, especially in uncertain economic times or when the company struggles financially. If the truth comes out, it can lead to loss of employee morale, increased resignations, and lawsuits for breach of contract or employment law violations.

Lying in economic contexts often has severe and far-reaching consequences for the individual or entity involved and the broader market, employees, consumers, and even entire economies. Lying in economic situations, particularly in financial markets, corporate governance, and public disclosures, can lead to serious legal consequences. These repercussions uphold trust and integrity in financial and corporate systems.

Here's a list of typical legal consequences that can arise from lying in various economic contexts:

Fines and Penalties – Individuals and companies caught lying in economic transactions or reports often face substantial fines. These penalties are imposed by regulatory bodies such as the Securities and Exchange Commission (SEC) in the United States or similar financial regulatory authorities worldwide. Fines serve both as punishment for the offending party and as a deterrent to discourage similar behavior by others.

Criminal Charges – In cases where lying involves fraud, insider trading, embezzlement, or other forms of financial deceit, criminal charges may be filed. This can lead to prosecution and, if found guilty, imprisonment. Criminal sanctions address severe dishonesty that not only breaches regulatory standards but also constitutes a violation of law.

Civil Lawsuits – Victims of economic deceit (such as investors, shareholders, or partners) may file civil lawsuits for damages caused by the lies. This could include compensation for financial losses, punitive damages, and other related costs. Civil actions aim to restore the financial position of the aggrieved parties as if the deceit had not occurred, thereby providing a remedy for the loss incurred.

Restitution and Disgorgement – Courts or regulatory bodies may order the perpetrator of economic lies to pay restitution to the victims or disgorge any profits gained from the dishonest activities. These measures ensure that wrongdoers do not profit from their fraudulent actions and that victims are compensated for their losses.

Revocation of Licenses or Certifications – Professionals found guilty of lying in economic roles—such as accountants, financial advisors, or corporate executives—may have their professional licenses or certifications revoked. This consequence prevents them from practicing in their field, protecting the public from future harm.

Bans from Serving in Directorial or Executive Positions – Individuals guilty of significant economic deceit may be barred from serving in managerial or directorial roles in publicly traded companies or financial institutions. This restriction helps maintain the integrity of corporate governance and protects investors and stakeholders from potential future malfeasance.

Market Exclusion Sanctions – Traders or companies caught engaging in deceptive practices like market manipulation may be banned from trading on certain exchanges or operating in certain financial markets. These sanctions protect the fairness and integrity of financial markets, ensuring a level playing field for all participants.

Forced Resignations and Termination of Employment – Corporate executives or board members who lie might be forced to resign or be terminated, even if they do not face criminal charges. Such actions can help restore public confidence in a company's management and can be a part of broader efforts to rehabilitate the company's public image.

Asset Freezes – In cases involving fraud or other severe economic crimes, authorities may freeze the accused's assets to prevent the dissipation of funds that could be used to compensate victims or pay fines. Asset freezes ensure that funds remain available for restitution and discourage the movement of illicit gains.

Credit and Banking Restrictions – Individuals convicted of economic dishonesty might face restrictions when securing loans, credit, or banking services, as their creditworthiness and trustworthiness are significantly diminished. These restrictions protect financial institutions from risk and serve as a deterrent against future dishonesty.

Negative Credit Reporting – Businesses and individuals involved in deceitful economic practices may have their actions reported to credit agencies, affecting their credit scores and their ability to secure future financing. Ensuring accurate credit reporting helps lenders assess risk more effectively and discourages deceit by attaching long-term financial consequences.

Public Censure and Reputational Damage – While not a legal consequence in the traditional sense, public censure from regulatory bodies or industry groups can have significant reputational impacts that are akin to formal legal penalties. Public condemnation warns the community and industry about dishonest individuals or entities, helping to prevent future engagements with them.

These legal consequences are crucial in maintaining regulatory compliance and ethical standards in economic activities. They serve to punish and deter wrongful actions, compensate victims, and uphold the overall integrity of financial systems.

Here are 12 celebrities who have been known to lie.

1. **Jussie Smollett** (Actor) – 2019 – Smollet faked a hate crime attack and falsely reported it to the police. Smollett was found guilty of lying to police and staging the incident for his personal publicity.

2. **Kim Kardashian** (Reality TV Star) – 2016 – Kardashian claimed Taylor Swift approved the controversial "Famous" lyrics by Kanye West. Swift denied approving the line, and leaked video footage later revealed that Swift had not agreed to the full context of the lyrics as portrayed.

3. **Brian Williams** (News Anchor) – 2015 – Williams falsely claimed to have been in a helicopter hit by an RPG (rocket-propelled grenade) during the Iraq War. Williams admitted he "misremembered" the event and was suspended from NBC News.

4. **Steve Rannazzisi** (Comedian) – 2015 – Rannazzisi claimed he was in the World Trade Center during the 9/11 attacks. He admitted the lie in 2015 after being confronted with evidence proving he wasn't in the towers.

5. **Rachel Dolezal** (Activist) – 2015 – Dolezal lied about being Black despite being born to white parents. Dolezal, a former NAACP chapter president, was outed by her parents and admitted to misrepresenting her race.

6. **Shia LaBeouf** (Actor) – 2013 – LaBeouf plagiarized Daniel Clowes' graphic novel for his short film and initially denied it. LaBeouf's plagiarism was widely exposed, and he later apologized for the incident on social media.

7. **Lance Armstrong** (Cyclist) – 1999-2012 – Armstrong denied using performance-enhancing drugs throughout his career. He admitted to doping in a 2013 interview with Oprah Winfrey after years of denial.

8. **Tiger Woods** (Golfer) – 2009 – Woods lied about his fidelity and involvement in multiple extramarital affairs. He publicly apologized for

his infidelities after a series of affairs became public, damaging his career and reputation.

9. **Martha Stewart** (Businesswoman) – 2001-2004 – Stewart lied about insider trading and obstructed justice during an investigation. She served time in prison after being convicted for lying about selling stock based on non-public information.

10. **Paris Hilton** (Socialite) – 2003 – Hilton claimed to have never used drugs despite multiple reports of drug use. Hilton was arrested for cocaine possession in 2010, which contradicted her earlier claims of abstaining from drugs.

11. **O.J. Simpson** (Former NFL Player) – 1995 – Simpson claimed innocence in the murder of Nicole Brown Simpson and Ron Goldman. Though Simpson was acquitted in the criminal trial, he was found liable for their deaths in a civil suit, leading many to believe he lied about his involvement.

12. **Milli Vanilli** (Music Duo) – 1990 – Milli Vanilli lip-synced their songs whereas session musicians performed the actual vocals. The scandal erupted after it was revealed that Rob Pilatus and Fab Morvan didn't sing on their Grammy-winning album.

These examples showcase how lies or dishonesty from celebrities can lead to legal repercussions, public backlash, and loss of reputation.

References

American Psychological Association. (n.d.). The role of honesty in interpersonal relationships. Retrieved from https://www.apa.org

Bok, S. (1999). Lying: Moral choice in public and private life. New York, NY: Vintage Books.

DePaulo, B. M., & Kashy, D. A. (1998). Everyday lies in close and casual relationships. Journal of Personality and Social Psychology, 74(1), 63–79. https://doi.org/10.1037/0022-3514.74.1.63

FactCheck.org. (n.d.). Combating misinformation in social and professional settings. Retrieved from https://www.factcheck.org

Goffman, E. (1959). The presentation of self in everyday life. Garden City, NY: Doubleday.

Lewandowsky, S., Ecker, U. K., & Cook, J. (2017). Beyond misinformation: Understanding and coping with the "post-truth" era. Journal of Applied Research in Memory and Cognition, 6(4), 353–369 https://doi.org/10.1016/j.jarmac.2017.07.008

Pennycook, G., & Rand, D. G. (2018). The Implied Truth Effect: Attaching warnings to a subset of fake news stories increases the perceived accuracy of stories without warnings. Management Science, 66(11), 4944 4957. https://doi.org/10.1287/mnsc.2019.3478

PolitiFact. (n.d.). Detecting lies and maintaining trust in professional settings. Retrieved from https://www.politifact.com

Rosenthal, R. (2002). The honesty gap: Social lying and its consequences. Cambridge, MA: Harvard University Press.

Snopes. (n.d.). Myth-busting in social and professional interactions. Retrieved from https://www.snopes.com

Vrij, A. (2008). Detecting lies and deceit: Pitfalls and opportunities (2nd ed.). Hoboken, NJ: Wiley.

Chapter Nine:
Economic Situations

Truth is a cornerstone of sound financial decision-making. Untruths, when they infiltrate an economic situation, can have far-reaching financial repercussions, affecting individuals, businesses, and entire economies. Economic decision-making, whether in markets, investments, or government policies, is heavily reliant on trust. False information can lead to poor decision-making, financial losses, and economic crises.

For individuals, the ability to discern economic untruths is crucial for making sound personal financial decisions. In navigating the often conflicting information, people will seek advice from financial advisors, media reports, and friends. While these sources can be helpful, it's important to remember that not all advice is based on sound reasoning or truth. Misleading information can lead individuals to make poor investments, take on unsustainable debt, or fall for financial scams. Understanding the truth behind economic claims helps individuals protect their wealth and plan for their futures more effectively.

In business, truthfulness is critical for maintaining fair and competitive markets. Companies that engage in deceptive practices, whether through false advertising or misleading financial reporting, can distort market dynamics. When companies misrepresent their performance or engage in fraudulent activities, it can lead to significant economic losses for investors, employees, and consumers. For example, large-scale corporate fraud, as seen in cases like Enron, left a trail of economic devastation. Its fraudulent activities—such as hiding debt and inflating profits, impacted energy trading, accounting, and corporate governance.

Enron pioneered energy trading, creating markets for electricity and gas. When the company collapsed, businesses and consumers reliant on its services faced uncertainty. The energy sector adapted and survived, bolstered by subsequent regulations. The scandal exposed vulnerabilities in how energy markets operated. The accounting and auditing industry faced a severe blow. Arthur Andersen, one of the "Big Five" accounting firms, was implicated in shredding documents and failing to catch Enron's fraud. Its collapse reduced the "Big Five" to the "Big Four" and shook public trust in auditors.

Investors and employees suffered significant losses. Enron's bankruptcy wiped out billions in shareholder value and devastated pension funds, leaving many workers without retirement savings. This created widespread skepticism about corporate governance. The fallout spurred regulatory reforms, most notably the Sarbanes-Oxley Act of 2002, which imposed stricter financial reporting and auditing standards to prevent similar scandals. Enron left a legacy of economic devastation, regulatory reform, and heightened awareness of the dangers of unchecked corporate greed and poor oversight. Its impact reshaped business practices and corporate accountability.

Economic policies are often influenced by the information available to decision-makers at the national and global levels. Misleading economic data or false claims about market trends can result in misguided policies, leading to recessions, inflation, or other adverse outcomes. However, with increased awareness and vigilance, citizens can prevent such misinformation from influencing policies. If governments base fiscal policies on incorrect data or analyses, they may implement strategies that exacerbate economic problems rather than alleviate them. Citizens must be vigilant about the accuracy of financial information and hold policymakers accountable for their decisions based on that information.

Spotting truth from untruth in political, social, and economic situations is vital for making informed decisions, fostering trust, and ensuring accountability at all levels of society. Without this discernment, falsehoods can take root, leading to widespread harm across all facets of life. With a culture of accountability, we can ensure that financial decisions are made with integrity and transparency, providing a sense of security and confidence to all stakeholders.

Here are twelve economic situations where lies or misrepresentations had an impact on investors, companies, and the industry:

1. **Wells Fargo Fake Accounts Scandal** – 2016 – Wells Fargo employees secretly opened millions of unauthorized accounts to meet sales targets without customers' knowledge or consent. The company was fined $185 million, and the scandal led to the resignation of its CEO.

2. **Theranos Scandal** – 2015 – Elizabeth Holmes falsely claimed that Theranos' blood-testing technology could perform hundreds of tests from a single drop of blood. Investigative reports revealed that the technology was unreliable, leading to the company's collapse and Holmes' conviction for fraud.

3. **Volkswagen Emissions Scandal ("Dieselgate")** – 2015 – Volkswagen falsely claimed their diesel vehicles met emissions standards while secretly installing defeat devices to cheat tests. VW admitted to the deception, leading to billions in fines and vehicle recalls.

4. **Libor Manipulation Scandal** – 2012 – Several banks, including Barclays, were caught manipulating the London Interbank Offered Rate (Libor) to profit from trades. Barclays paid $450 million in fines, and the scandal affected trust in the global financial system.

5. **Satyam Scandal** – 2009 – Indian IT company Satyam falsely inflated its revenue and profits by $1.5 billion, deceiving shareholders. The company's chairman admitted to the fraud, leading to his arrest and collapse.

6. **AIG Financial Products Fraud** –2008 – AIG misled investors about the risk exposure of its credit default swaps, leading to its near-collapse and a $182 billion government bailout. AIG's role in the financial crisis is well-documented, and its bailout was highly controversial.

7. **Bernie Madoff Ponzi Scheme** – 2008 – Bernie Madoff falsely promised high returns on investments in a Ponzi scheme, deceiving thousands of investors for years. Madoff was sentenced to 150 years in prison after defrauding investors of around $65 billion.

8. **Lehman Brothers Collapse** – 2008 – Lehman Brothers used an accounting trick called "Repo 105" to hide the true extent of their liabilities before the financial collapse. The firm's bankruptcy was one of the major catalysts of the global financial crisis.

9. **Fannie Mae and Freddie Mac Accounting Scandal** – 2004 – Fannie Mae and Freddie Mac executives misrepresented the crisis.

Both companies were placed under government conservatorship after the 2008 financial crisis revealed widespread mismanagement.

10. **HealthSouth Accounting Fraud** – 2003 – HealthSouth executives inflated earnings by $2.7 billion to meet Wall Street expectations, deceiving investors for years. The CEO was acquitted of criminal charges, but the company faced lawsuits and financial ruin.

11. **WorldCom Accounting Fraud** – 2002 – WorldCom inflated its assets by $11 billion through fraudulent accounting practices, making the company appear more profitable. WorldCom's bankruptcy became one of the largest accounting scandals in U.S. history.

12. **Enron Scandal** – 2001 – Enron executives used accounting loopholes to hide billions in debt from failed deals and projects, misleading investors. Enron declared bankruptcy in 2001, and its executives were charged with fraud and conspiracy.

These examples illustrate how economic lies and fraud have far-reaching consequences, often leading to financial loss, legal penalties, and public distrust.

Lying in economic situations, whether by individuals, businesses, or governments, involves deliberate dishonesty or misinformation to gain financial advantage.

While lying might bring short-term gains, the long-term consequences can be severe, affecting both the liar and the more extensive economic system.

1. **Misrepresenting Financial Statements** (Fraud) - Companies or individuals may falsify records, inflate revenue, or understate liabilities to appear more financially stable. If uncovered, it leads to legal repercussions, loss of investor trust, and potential business collapse. Examples include Enron and Bernie Madoff's Ponzi scheme.

2. **Deceptive Advertising and Sales** - Misleading customers about product value, quality, or scarcity. Loss of consumer trust, potential

lawsuits, and regulatory action. Long-term damage to brand reputation can hurt future profitability.

3. **Insider Trading or Market Manipulation** - Using non-public information or creating false impressions in financial markets to make illegal gains. Heavy legal penalties, imprisonment, and a significant impact on market integrity, can cause losses to other investors and affect market stability.

4. **Lying in Job Applications** (Credentials/Salary) - Individuals may lie about qualifications or previous salaries to secure higher-paying jobs or positions of power. If discovered, it can lead to job loss, reputational harm, and difficulty finding future employment.

5. **Government Manipulation of Economic Data** - Governments might falsify economic statistics (e.g., inflation, GDP growth) to paint a more favorable picture of the economy. When the truth emerges, it can lead to a loss of credibility, decreased foreign investment, currency devaluation, and even social unrest.

Consequences of Economic Lies:

1. **Legal Repercussions:** Lying in financial contexts often leads to criminal charges, civil lawsuits, fines, or imprisonment. Regulatory bodies like the SEC in the U.S. strictly monitor economic behavior.

2. **Loss of Trust:** Lying erodes trust, whether in personal relationships, business, or with the public. This can lead to a collapse in customer or investor confidence, reduced business opportunities, and reputational damage.

3. **Market Instability:** Lies in financial markets can cause sudden market corrections, panics, and long-term instability as misinformation gets corrected, leading to losses for honest participants.

4. **Moral and Ethical Consequences:** Lying creates moral and ethical dilemmas beyond legal and financial impacts. A culture of dishonesty can spread, leading to broader corruption within systems or institutions.

5. **Long-Term Economic Damage:** Lies can cause long-term harm to economies by distorting accurate economic health indicators, making it challenging to address underlying problems. For example, a country hiding inflation data might fail to implement monetary policies to stabilize the economy.

While economic lying might provide a short-term benefit, the eventual costs—legal, reputational, financial, and systemic—are generally far higher.

References

American Institute of Certified Public Accountants (AICPA). (n.d.). The importance of ethical financial reporting. Retrieved from https://www.aicpa.org

Bok, S. (1999). Lying: Moral choice in public and private life. New York, NY: Vintage Books.

Enron Corp. (2001). Enron scandal and corporate fraud: A case study. Retrieved from https://www.sec.gov

Gaughan, P. A. (2010). Mergers, acquisitions, and corporate restructurings (5th ed.). Hoboken, NJ: Wiley.

Investopedia. (n.d.). Ponzi schemes and financial frauds: Key cases. Retrieved from https://www.investopedia.com

Morris, C. R. (2008). The trillion dollar meltdown: Easy money, high rollers, and the great credit crash. New York, NY: PublicAffairs.

Petersen, T., & Schoenfeld, H. (2007). Business ethics and the impact of corporate scandals on investor confidence. Journal of Business Ethics, 72(2), 211–220. https://doi.org/10.1007/s10551-006-9161-9

PolitiFact. (n.d.). Verifying claims in economic and financial policy debates. Retrieved from https://www.politifact.com

Snopes. (n.d.). Fact-checking economic misinformation and corporate claims. Retrieved from https://www.snopes.com

Sorkin, A. R. (2010). Too big to fail: The inside story of how Wall Street and Washington fought to save the financial system—and themselves. New York, NY: Viking.

Stiglitz, J. E. (2012). The price of inequality: How today's divided society endangers our future. New York, NY: W.W. Norton & Company.

The Economist. (n.d.). Corporate fraud and economic stability. Retrieved from https://www.economist.com

Chapter Ten:
Deterring Dishonesty

Deterring dishonesty involves cultivating environments across personal, business, and societal contexts where honesty is both valued and consistently rewarded and where the potential consequences of lying significantly outweigh any perceived short-term gains. In personal relationships, fostering open communication creates safe spaces for truthfulness, while positive reinforcement, such as acknowledging and appreciating honesty, strengthens trust and mutual respect.

Role modeling ethical behavior, particularly by parents and mentors, teaches the next generation the importance of integrity as a cornerstone of strong and meaningful connections. Within businesses, these principles are essential for establishing an ethical corporate culture. Transparency in operations, accountability through clear policies, and leadership by example encourage employees to prioritize truthfulness and integrity in their professional conduct.

Positive reinforcement, such as recognizing ethical behavior in performance evaluations and team meetings, builds a workplace where honesty is a key value, while clear and consistent consequences for dishonesty, such as disciplinary actions for fraudulent behavior, deter unethical practices. In schools, communities, and broader societal systems, educating individuals about the value of honesty, creating supportive environments for ethical decision-making, and enforcing fair and transparent consequences for dishonest actions cultivate a culture of integrity.

Public figures, educators, and leaders who model honesty have a profound influence on societal norms, reinforcing the expectation of ethical behavior. By embedding these practices into every aspect of life, from personal interactions to institutional frameworks, individuals are more likely to act truthfully, strengthening trust and ethical standards across all levels of society.

The foundation of honesty lies in open, transparent communication. This approach not only discourages lying but also fosters a culture of trust and understanding, enhancing relationships and productivity. To foster this, creating an environment where individuals can speak openly without fear of severe judgment or punishment is essential. This is particularly crucial in settings like workplaces, schools, or family environments where honesty's stakes may be high.

Establishing "safe spaces" for truth-telling encourages people to speak their minds and admit mistakes without feeling that they will face extreme consequences. For example, in a professional setting, creating forums where employees can share their concerns or confess errors without retribution will foster a sense of trust. Similarly, in personal relationships, people are more inclined to tell the truth if they know their honesty will be met with understanding, even if the truth is uncomfortable.

Honest communication is a powerful tool for reducing misunderstandings and fostering openness. When regular, candid conversations are encouraged, people feel less pressure to lie to cover up mistakes or avoid conflict. Implementing regular check-ins or open-door policies in workplaces and families helps keep the lines of communication open, reducing the likelihood that individuals will feel the need to hide the truth.

Here are six methods that can help to ensure open communication within a group or organization:

1. **Team meetings** - Schedule consistent meetings where team members can share updates, concerns, and feedback in a structured setting. This encourages open dialogue and allows everyone to voice their opinions.

2. **Open-door policies**—Create an environment where employees feel comfortable approaching management with their thoughts and concerns. This fosters trust and encourages spontaneous conversations.

3. **Feedback channels**—Implement various feedback channels, such as anonymous suggestion boxes, online surveys, or digital platforms, to allow employees to share their ideas or concerns without fear of judgment.

4. **Training workshops** - Conduct communication skills training or workshops that emphasize the importance of honesty and transparency in interactions. This will equip employees with the tools to communicate effectively.

5.   **Conflict resolution processes**—Establish clear procedures for addressing organizational conflicts and misunderstandings. A structured approach encourages individuals to communicate openly about issues.

6.   **Informal social events** - Organize informal gatherings such as team-building or social events. These events allow employees to interact in a relaxed setting, which can promote openness and strengthen relationships.

Incentivizing honesty through positive reinforcement is one of the most effective strategies for encouraging truthful behavior. When individuals see that telling the truth results in tangible benefits, they are more likely to act with integrity. This can be done in both personal and professional settings.

It would be usual to publicly acknowledge honesty as a powerful motivator, as it aligns with common practices in personal and professional settings where integrity is highly valued. Recognizing honesty reinforces desirable behavior and builds trust, which is essential for effective relationships and organizational success. However, coupling honesty with tangible rewards, such as promotions or bonuses, is somewhat less common and might be seen as unusual, depending on the workplace culture. While this approach could enhance motivation and trust, there's a risk that it might inadvertently shift honesty from being an intrinsic value to a transactional behavior.

Another effective way to incentivize honesty is to establish trust-based systems. Individuals known for their honesty can be granted more freedom and flexibility, such as flexible working hours or greater autonomy in decision-making. This approach clearly demonstrates that honesty leads to increased independence, further encouraging truthful behavior.

Transparency is vital in any system. People are more likely to act with integrity when they see that honest behavior is rewarded and that the consequences of dishonesty are predictable.

Ensuring that rewards for honesty apply equally to everyone, without favoritism, helps build a culture where truthfulness is the norm rather than the exception.

1.   **Surveys and questionnaires** - Conduct regular surveys to assess employees' perceptions of honesty and integrity within the organization and their views on the effectiveness of positive reinforcement strategies.

2. **Employee feedback sessions** - Hold focus groups or feedback sessions where employees can discuss their experiences with positive reinforcement and its influence on their behavior and attitudes toward honesty.

3. **Performance metrics** - Analyze changes in performance metrics, such as error rates or the incidence of dishonesty, before and after implementing positive reinforcement strategies to determine their effectiveness.

4. **Retention rates** - Monitor employee retention and turnover rates, as an increase in honesty and integrity may lead to higher job satisfaction and reduced turnover, indicating a positive workplace culture.

5. **Incident reports** - Track the frequency of dishonesty-related incidents or violations within the organization over time to see if implemented reinforcement policies reduce such occurrences.

6. **Recognition programs evaluation** - Assess the participation and outcomes of recognition programs related to honest behavior, including how often employees are acknowledged for their honesty and whether this correlates with changes in their behavior.

To effectively deter dishonesty, transparent and fair consequences must be in place for those who lie. When people understand the potential repercussions of lying, they are likelier to choose honesty. However, these consequences must be communicated upfront and enforced consistently to be effective.

Setting clear expectations from the outset is essential. Everyone should understand the standards of behavior and what constitutes dishonesty, whether in a workplace, family, or social group. An employee handbook or code of conduct can outline the specific consequences of dishonesty in professional settings. In families, open discussions about the importance of honesty and the repercussions of lying can help set the stage for truthful interactions.

A tiered system of consequences can be particularly effective. Minor infractions lead to lighter consequences, while repeated or severe dishonesty results in more significant penalties. For example, a first offense might result in a verbal warning, while repeated offenses could lead to more serious actions such as suspensions or loss of privileges.

Consistency in enforcing these consequences is critical. If people see that the rules are applied fairly and equally to everyone, regardless of their position or relationship, they are more likely to respect the system. This fairness in the system can help build trust and discourage dishonesty, as individuals understand that everyone is held to the same standard, promoting a sense of justice.

Providing opportunities for redemption is also essential. When someone admits to dishonesty or makes a mistake, offering a chance to make amends—such as through an apology or corrective action—reinforces the idea that truthfulness is valued, even after an error. Reduced consequences for those who come forward with the truth before being caught can encourage honest behavior, promoting a sense of compassion in the system.

Promoting Ethical Role Models and Leadership

Leaders play a crucial role in promoting honesty by modeling ethical behavior. When those in positions of authority, whether in a workplace, school, or family, demonstrate integrity, it sets a powerful example for others to follow. This influence of leadership can significantly impact the culture of honesty in an organization or community.

In professional settings, rewarding and promoting leaders who consistently act with transparency and integrity sends a clear message that honesty is valued at all levels. Highlighting these leaders as role models helps set the tone for the organization.

Sharing success stories of honesty can also inspire others. Whether through case studies, real-life examples, or public recognition of individuals who acted with integrity, these stories can demonstrate the real-world benefits of truthfulness. In the workplace, this might mean showcasing how an honest employee avoided more significant issues by addressing a problem early, while in personal relationships, it could mean celebrating the trust that comes from consistent honesty.

Peer accountability can further strengthen a culture of honesty. Encouraging recognition programs where peers nominate each other for acts of integrity helps build a community where truthfulness is the norm. For example, a "truth-teller" award in a workplace or social group can encourage individuals to prioritize honesty.

Group incentives for collective honesty can also be effective. In team settings, rewarding the entire group for demonstrating transparency and integrity helps foster a sense of shared responsibility. This could be through improved team performance, increased trust, or shared rewards for collective honesty.

Often, people lie out of fear of punishment. Reducing the severity of consequences for those who admit their mistakes before being caught can encourage more truthful behavior. When people know that admitting a mistake will result in less severe repercussions than if caught lying, they are more likely to come forward.

This can be achieved by creating a culture where mistakes are seen as opportunities for growth and learning rather than something to be punished harshly. In professional and personal settings, understanding and leniency for those who tell the truth can reinforce the idea that honesty is always the better choice, even in difficult situations. It's essential to highlight the long-term benefits of honesty. Trust, once earned, leads to stronger relationships, whether in the workplace, family, or friendships. When individuals see that honesty builds lasting bonds, they are more likely to value it. A reputation for integrity can open doors to future opportunities, career advancements, and deeper personal connections.

Reinforcing the idea that an honest reputation can lead to better prospects helps shift the focus from short-term gains to long-term success. In a professional context, individuals who consistently demonstrate honesty are likelier to be trusted with leadership roles or given greater responsibilities. In personal relationships, being known as a reliable and truthful person fosters deeper connections and strengthens bonds over time.

Ongoing feedback is crucial for reinforcing the value of honesty. Whether in the workplace, at home, or in social settings, regularly acknowledging honest behavior helps individuals understand its positive impact. Providing feedback on how truthfulness improves relationships, builds trust, or solves problems encourages people to continue being truthful.

Sometimes, people avoid honesty because they don't know how to communicate complex truths effectively. Offering guidance and teaching communication skills, such as tactfully framing an uncomfortable truth, can make it easier for individuals to embrace honesty. This reduces the fear of negative repercussions and helps build confidence in handling sensitive situations with integrity.

Establishing transparent and fair processes in any environment is important to further deter dishonesty. When individuals understand how honesty is rewarded and what consequences they face for lying, they are more likely to choose the former. In a professional setting, for instance, clearly outlining the rewards for integrity and the penalties for dishonesty in an employee handbook ensures that everyone is on the same page.

Transparency also involves avoiding favoritism. When rewards or consequences are applied equally and fairly to all, people are more inclined to trust the system. If honesty is rewarded only for a select few or consequences are enforced inconsistently, it creates room for distrust, and individuals may be tempted to lie to protect themselves.

People often lie to meet unrealistic expectations or avoid harsh consequences. Reducing this pressure can create a more honest environment. In workplaces, lowering the pressure to meet unattainable goals can reduce the temptation to fabricate results or hide mistakes. In personal relationships, allowing room for imperfection and normalizing the idea that mistakes are part of learning and growth reduces the need to lie to save face.

When individuals feel they won't be harshly judged for admitting their faults, they are more likely to act truthfully. Encouraging a culture that values progress and personal growth over perfection allows people to be more open about their challenges rather than resorting to dishonesty to avoid disappointment.

Educating people about the long-term consequences of dishonesty is an effective deterrent. Lying erodes trust and can have serious personal, professional, and even legal ramifications. When individuals understand how dishonesty damages relationships, reputations, and mental health, they are more likely to think twice before lying.

In personal relationships, dishonesty often leads to feelings of guilt, anxiety, and isolation as individuals struggle to maintain their lies. Professionally, lies can result in loss of credibility, disciplinary action, or even termination. In legal situations, dishonesty can lead to criminal charges such as perjury or fraud. Using real-life examples or case studies to illustrate these consequences can make the abstract idea of dishonesty's harm more tangible and relatable.

Encouraging empathy is also crucial. Teaching individuals to put themselves in the shoes of those affected by lies helps them understand the emotional and practical harm caused by dishonesty. When people realize the ripple effect that their lies can have—damaging trust, causing misunderstandings, or even harming others—they may be more inclined to choose honesty.

Building a culture where trust is the foundation of relationships—whether in the workplace, family, or social groups—creates a positive feedback loop where honesty becomes the default expectation. People are more likely to act with integrity when they trust that others will do the same. Encouraging mutual trust involves promoting transparency in all interactions through honest feedback systems or open discussions.

Incorporating peer accountability into this culture further strengthens the commitment to honesty. In a workplace setting, implementing programs where peers recognize each other's acts of integrity can reinforce the collective value placed on truthfulness. When groups hold each other accountable, the pressure to lie diminishes, and honesty becomes a shared responsibility.

Here are a few examples of programs that have helped to promote a culture of honesty:

1. **Whistleblower protection programs** - Many organizations, including corporations and government agencies, have implemented whistleblower protection initiatives that encourage employees to report unethical behavior without fear of retaliation, fostering an environment of honesty.

2. **Integrity and ethics programs** - Companies like Boeing and Deloitte have established comprehensive training programs focused on ethics and integrity, guiding employees on the importance of honesty and the impacts of their actions.

3. **Open communication programs** - Organizations such as Buffer have adopted transparent communication tools, allowing all employees access to information, and encouraging open dialogue, which promotes honesty and accountability.

4. **Employee recognition systems** - The software company HubSpot has a values-based recognition program that rewards employees for

exemplifying honesty and integrity, reinforcing the importance of these traits within the company culture.

5. **Failure-focused initiatives** - Google practices a "blameless post-mortem" approach. This methodology involves analyzing mistakes openly without assigning blame to individuals. By fostering an environment where employees can discuss errors candidly, Google encourages learning and continuous improvement, reducing the likelihood of repeated incidents. This approach is a critical component of Google's Site Reliability Engineering (SRE) practices, promoting a culture of transparency and resilience.

6. **Ethics ombudsman programs** - Many educational institutions, such as universities, have established ethics officers or ombudsman programs that provide a safe space for students and staff to report unethical behavior, thus promoting a culture of transparency and honesty.

Deterring dishonesty requires more than just setting rules and consequences—it involves creating a comprehensive environment where honesty is consistently valued, rewarded, and modeled. You foster open communication, incentivize truthfulness, establish clear consequences, and promote ethical leadership. Regular feedback, peer accountability, and trust-based systems all contribute to an environment where the benefits of honesty far outweigh the temptation to lie.

In the long run, building a culture of integrity helps individuals understand the importance of honesty for immediate success and for creating lasting, trustworthy relationships in both personal and professional life.

References

American Psychological Association. (n.d.). Promoting honesty and integrity: The psychological principles behind ethical behavior. Retrieved from https://www.apa.org

Bazerman, M. H., & Tenbrunsel, A. E. (2011). Blind spots: Why we fail to do what's right and what to do about it. Princeton, NJ: Princeton University Press.

Bok, S. (1999). Lying: Moral choice in public and private life. New York, NY: Vintage Books.

DePaulo, B. M., & Kashy, D. A. (1998). Everyday lies in close and casual relationships. Journal of Personality and Social Psychology, 74(1), 63–79. https://doi.org/10.1037/0022-3514.74.1.63

Goleman, D. (1995). Emotional intelligence: Why it can matter more than IQ. New York, NY: Bantam Books.

Levine, T. R. (2014). Truth-default theory (TDT): A theory of human deception and deception detection. Journal of Language and Social Psychology, 33(4), 378–392. https://doi.org/10.1177/0261927X14535916

PolitiFact. (n.d.). Strategies to promote transparency and reduce dishonesty in organizations. Retrieved from https://www.politifact.com

Rosenthal, R. (2002). The honesty gap: Social lying and its consequences. Cambridge, MA: Harvard University Press.

Snopes. (n.d.). Understanding and deterring dishonesty in personal and professional contexts. Retrieved from https://www.snopes.com

Trevino, L. K., & Nelson, K. A. (2016). Managing business ethics: Straight talk about how to do it right (7th ed.). Hoboken, NJ: Wiley.

Wardle, C., & Derakhshan, H. (2017). Information disorder: Toward an interdisciplinary framework for research and policymaking. Council of Europe. Retrieved from https://www.coe.int

Whitney, D. K., & Trosten-Bloom, A. (2010). The power of appreciative inquiry: A practical guide to positive change (2nd ed.). Oakland, CA: Berrett-Koehler Publishers.

Chapter Eleven:
Believe and Disbelieve

The lights dim in the debate hall, and the candidates walk onto the stage, shaking hands before taking their positions behind gleaming podiums. As the audience buzzes with anticipation, another type of preparation occurs behind the scenes in newsrooms, media offices, and fact- checking centers nationwide. The stakes are high. Voters will be swayed by what the candidates say tonight, and it's up to a team of professionals — journalists, researchers, and real-time systems — to ensure that the public knows what is true, what is half-true, and what is utterly false. The fact-checkers are ready for action.

Fact-checking during a political debate is complex. It involves several critical steps each designed to capture the accuracy of the candidates' claims and promptly deliver verified information to the public. Understanding this process can help viewers appreciate the effort behind the scenes to maintain the integrity of the democratic process.

The Preparation Phase

Long before the debate begins, fact-checkers are already hard at work, demonstrating their unwavering dedication. Their job starts with extensive research on the candidates. Fact-checking organizations study past statements, policy proposals, voting records, and public claims made by each individual on stage. The goal is to anticipate what topics might come up during the debate and be ready with the facts.

Take, for example, a debate on healthcare reform. Fact-checkers will have reviewed vital policy positions on this issue for each candidate, including their public speeches, legislative history, and campaign promises. This preparation allows them to respond quickly when candidates bring up claims—whether it's about the affordability of universal healthcare or the success of a specific policy.

Another crucial tool in the fact-checkers' arsenal is their database. Major fact-checking organizations, such as FactCheck.org, PolitiFact, and The Washington Post Fact Checker, maintain extensive databases of verified facts on various issues, including economics, foreign policy, healthcare, climate change, and more. These databases allow them to cross-reference claims made during the debate with previously verified information in real-time.

Real-Time Fact-Checking

When the debate begins, fact-checkers engage in real-time analysis. It's a fast-paced, intense process where every word is scrutinized. Teams of fact-checkers sit in front of screens, listening closely to each statement, focusing on critical claims made by the candidates.

Imagine a candidate who claims that crime rates have skyrocketed under the current administration. The fact-checkers will immediately compare that statement to crime statistics from official sources like the FBI's Uniform Crime Reporting (UCR) Program. They can quickly verify whether the claim is accurate or exaggerated using online research tools.

This process isn't just about speed, though. It's also about collaboration. Most fact-checking teams work with experts in different fields — economics, law, healthcare, and environmental policy — who can offer specialized knowledge to assess the accuracy of claims. This collaborative effort ensures that the most accurate information is presented to the public.

Some organizations also rely on real-time fact-checking software that helps flag statements likely to be false or misleading based on past claims. These tools can assist fact-checkers by identifying claims that have already been debunked or tracking statistics that politicians frequently manipulate.

However, real-time fact-checking could be better. The speed required to verify information during a debate can sometimes limit the depth of analysis. That's why many organizations follow up with more detailed, post-debate analyses.

Here are some of the methods fact-checking organizations use to verify claims in real-time during a debate:

1. Cross-referencing claims with databases of verified facts.

2. Consulting existing research papers or articles related to the claim.

3. Utilizing live statistics from reliable sources like government databases and reports.

4. Accessing news archives to check past statements made by candidates.

5. Engaging experts in relevant fields for immediate insights.

6. Employing real-time fact-checking software to flag potentially false statements.

7. Monitoring social media for additional context or previously debunked claims.

8. Analyzing official reports from agencies like the FBI or CDC.

9. Checking academic studies that pertain to the topic discussed.

10. Utilizing tools like Google Fact Check Explorer to find information quickly.

11. Reviewing historical data on the relevant issue to provide context.

12. Collaborating with other fact-checking organizations to verify information across multiple sources.

Fact-checkers determine which claims are most critical to check during a debate by considering several factors:

1. **Relevance to key issues** - They focus on claims related to major topics of discussion, such as healthcare, the economy, or foreign policy, as these are often pivotal for voters.

2. **Frequency of claims** - Claims repeated frequently by candidates or aligned with familiar narratives in the election cycle are prioritized.

3. **Potential impact on voters** - Fact-checkers assess which statements could significantly influence public opinion or voter behavior, thus warranting closer scrutiny.

4. **Controversial or polarizing statements** - Claims likely to provoke debate or are highly polarizing often receive heightened attention due to their potential implications.

5. **Previous history** - Past statements made by candidates are reviewed to identify patterns of misinformation, focusing on those with a history of inaccurate claims.

6. **Expert input** - Collaborating with subject matter experts helps fact-checkers identify essential claims that require specialized knowledge for accurate verification.

7. **Audience engagement** - They may analyze social media trends or audience questions to determine which claims generate the most discussion or concern among viewers.

By using these criteria, fact-checkers aim to ensure their efforts focus on the most impactful and critical claims during debates.

Fact-checkers face several challenges in ensuring accuracy while working under tight time constraints during debates:

1. **Limited time for research** - The rapid pace of debates leaves little time for thorough verification of claims, forcing fact-checkers to make quick decisions on what to validate.

2. **Volume of claims** - Numerous statements can be made quickly, making it difficult to prioritize which require immediate attention.

3. **Complexity of issues** - Many topics discussed can be multifaceted or technical, requiring in-depth knowledge and careful analysis that is hard to achieve quickly.

4. **Information overload** - Accessing and sorting through abundant information from various sources in real time can be overwhelming and lead to potential errors.

5. **Coordination among team members** - Keeping a fact-checking team aligned and efficient under pressure can be challenging, especially when handling different claims simultaneously.

6. **Communication constraints** - Communicating accurate information to the audience in a timely manner can be difficult, especially when corrections need to be prepared on short notice.

7. **Unreliable sources** - Some statements may be based on data from questionable or misleading sources, complicating the verification process.

8. **Potential for misinterpretation** - Quick assessments may lead to misunderstandings of candidates' meanings, which can result in misleading conclusions or inaccuracies.

9. **Media pressure** - The expectation for immediate updates and fact-checks can create pressure to produce results quickly, sometimes at the expense of thoroughness.

10. **Evolving narrative** - Candidates may change their positions during the debate, leading to confusion and requiring fact-checkers to adapt their strategies rapidly.

These challenges underscore the complexity of real-time fact-checking in a high-stakes environment like a political debate.

Post-Debate Verification

Once the debate ends, the fact-checking process continues. In this phase, fact-checkers dive deeper into the claims made on stage, consulting additional experts, government reports, academic studies, and other credible sources to ensure their evaluations are as accurate and thorough as possible.

If a candidate claims that a particular policy saved millions of dollars, fact-checkers will investigate the source of that statistic, reviewing government spending reports or economic analyses to determine whether the number is correct and presented in the proper context.

The results of this post-debate analysis are often published in detailed fact-check articles. Media organizations may rate the claims using systems like "true," "half-true," or "false." These ratings help the public quickly gauge the validity of the statements made during the debate. PolitiFact's "Truth-O-Meter" offers visual feedback, with ratings like "Pants on Fire" for claims that are not just false but absurd.

In today's digital age, fact-checking doesn't just happen in the newsroom. It also plays out in real time on television screens and social media platforms. During televised debates, viewers may see fact-checks appear as graphics or text boxes that immediately signal whether a claim is accurate. These real- time visual aids let viewers stay informed without waiting for post-debate reports.

Social media has become another essential platform for fact-checking. Fact-checking organizations post updates on Twitter, Facebook, and other social platforms to engage with the public during debates. This makes the information more accessible and empowers viewers to quickly assess the truthfulness of what they're hearing. A viewer watching a discussion can follow along with live fact-checking feeds, ensuring false claims don't mislead them.

This process of fact-checking, while complex, plays a crucial role in maintaining the integrity of the political debate. But even with professional fact-checkers on the job, how does a viewer know who to believe during a discussion? The answer lies in applying critical thinking and using reliable strategies to navigate the flood of information.

How Viewers Can Assess Credibility During a Debate

During a political debate, it's easy to be swayed by a candidate's charisma, eloquence, or even emotional appeals. However, determining who to believe requires a more analytical approach.

Rely on Independent Fact-Checkers – Following reputable fact-checking organizations is a viewer's first defense against misinformation. Organizations like FactCheck.org, PolitiFact, and The Washington Post Fact Checker provide real-time and post-debate assessments. These groups have built their reputation on non-partisan, rigorous analysis, helping viewers differentiate between accurate statements and misleading rhetoric. After hearing a claim, viewers can cross-check it with multiple credible sources, such as government reports, academic research, or previously published fact- checks. This provides an extra layer of verification beyond trusting what is said on stage.

Look for Consistency – One of the most telling signs of a candidate's credibility is consistency. Candidates who change positions frequently or contradict themselves during a debate should raise red flags. Voters can track past statements and positions to determine whether the candidate's current claims align with their previous rhetoric. Evasive responses are another sign to watch for. When candidates dodge direct questions or deflect the conversation, it might indicate they're attempting to avoid revealing the truth or confronting a complex issue.

Pay Attention to Non-Verbal Cues – Body language, tone, and facial expressions can offer subtle clues about sincerity, as overconfidence or excessive emotional appeals may mask weak arguments or false information. By

110

contrast, a calm, consistent delivery often indicates that a person is speaking truthfully or is at least confident in their facts.

Be Aware of Bias – Confirmation bias is the tendency to favor information that confirms one's preexisting beliefs and is a challenge for any viewer. Recognizing this bias and remaining open to opposing viewpoints or corrections from fact-checkers is essential. Analyzing the language used by candidates can help viewers cut through emotional or manipulative rhetoric and focus on the substance of their claims.

Consider the Credibility of Sources – When candidates reference studies, experts, or statistics, it's essential to consider the source. Are these sources reputable, non-partisan, and credible? If a candidate relies on fringe sources or cherry-picks data, it could indicate that their claim is unreliable.

Watch for Oversimplification – Political issues are rarely simple, and when candidates offer overly simplistic solutions, it's worth questioning how realistic their proposals are. Sound-bite answers may need more depth to address the complexities of the issue.

Fact-checking during a political debate is a multi-layered process that involves careful preparation, real-time verification, and post-debate analysis. It ensures that the public can separate fact from fiction in politics' often fast-paced, emotional world. However, viewers also play a crucial role in this process. By following fact-checkers, paying attention to consistency and non-verbal cues, and thinking critically about the information presented, they can form well-informed opinions, helping democracy thrive.

References

American Press Institute. (n.d.). The role of fact-checking in political debates. Retrieved from https://www.americanpressinstitute.org

FactCheck.org. (n.d.). About us: How FactCheck.org verifies political claims. Retrieved from https://www.factcheck.org

Graves, L. (2016). Deciding what's true: The rise of political fact-checking in American journalism. New York, NY: Columbia University Press.

Kessler, G., Rizzo, S., & Kelly, M. (2019). The Washington Post Fact Checker: Trump's first 100 days. Washington, DC: Washington Post Press.

Lewandowsky, S., Ecker, U. K., & Cook, J. (2017). Beyond misinformation: Understanding and coping with the "post-truth" era. Journal of Applied Research in Memory and Cognition, 6(4), 353–369. https://doi.org/10.1016/j.jarmac.2017.07.008

PolitiFact. (n.d.). About the Truth-O-Meter: How PolitiFact rates claims. Retrieved from https://www.politifact.com

Snopes. (n.d.). How Snopes approaches real-time fact-checking. Retrieved from https://www.snopes.com

Wardle, C., & Derakhshan, H. (2017). Information disorder: Toward an interdisciplinary framework for research and policymaking. Council of Europe. Retrieved from https://www.coe.int

Zaller, J. R. (1992). The nature and origins of mass opinion. New York, NY: Cambridge University Press.

Chapter Twelve:
Conclusion

Distinguishing between truth and untruth is fundamental to understanding our world, fostering meaningful relationships, and making informed decisions. Truth serves as a compass, guiding us toward clarity, trust, and ethical living, while untruth obscures our way, often leading to confusion, distrust, and unintended harm.

When individuals rely on truth, they gain the ability to make decisions that are grounded. This empowerment instills a sense of confidence and security. Consider the example of a doctor diagnosing a patient. Accurate diagnostic information enables the doctor to prescribe an effective treatment, potentially saving a life. Conversely, information or incomplete data could lead to misdiagnosis, inappropriate treatment, and potentially severe consequences for the patient. In such scenarios, truth is not merely a virtue— it is a necessity that directly impacts lives.

In relationships, truth is essential for building and maintaining trust. Imagine a friendship where honesty prevails; both friends feel secure in their interactions, knowing they share genuine feelings and experiences. Compare this to a relationship where one friend frequently tells small lies. Over time, these falsehoods accumulate, eroding trust and leaving the deceived friend in constant doubt. Even truthful statements may be questioned, as trust, once broken, is exceedingly difficult to repair.

Truth aligns with a broader sense of moral integrity, shaping our actions and character. A student taking an exam faces a choice: answer honestly or cheat. Even when uncertain, honesty upholds their integrity and fosters genuine learning. This emphasis on genuine learning can inspire and motivate the audience. Conversely, cheating might provide temporary success but compromises their character and denies them the opportunity to grow through their mistakes.

In the realm of justice, truth serves as the cornerstone for fairness. Picture a courtroom where evidence and testimonies are presented. If a witness lies or evidence is manipulated, it can lead to the wrongful conviction of an innocent person. Justice relies on truth to ensure that the guilty are held accountable and the innocent are protected. Untruth undermines this process, perpetuating injustices that can have lifelong repercussions.

Even in less dramatic scenarios, untruth can cause significant harm. Misinformation, particularly in critical areas like healthcare, illustrates this point. For instance, if a myth misleads a patient about a miracle cure, they may forgo evidence-based treatments, endangering their health. Such harm may not be deliberate, but it underscores the tangible risks of misinformation.

Society can effectively combat misinformation in critical areas like healthcare through several key strategies. Firstly, increasing public awareness and education about media literacy can empower individuals to evaluate information sources and recognize bias or misinformation critically.

Secondly, healthcare organizations and professionals should actively communicate accurate information through trusted channels, such as community outreach, social media campaigns, and public health announcements. Clear and transparent communication can help build trust and dispel myths.

Additionally, fostering collaboration between governments, healthcare providers, and technology companies can enhance the monitoring of misinformation online. By implementing fact-checking mechanisms and promoting accurate health information, these entities can limit the spread of falsehoods.

Encouraging doctors and healthcare professionals to address patients' concerns and questions about misinformation actively can also be effective. By creating open dialogues, they can correct misunderstandings and provide reliable information.

Promoting supportive policies that prioritize credible health communication in public health strategies can ensure the consistent and reliable dissemination of accurate information.

Individuals can use several strategies to discern truth from untruth in everyday situations. Critical thinking is essential; questioning the sources of information and considering the evidence presented can help assess credibility. Seeking information from multiple reliable sources can provide a broader perspective and confirm facts.

Understanding the difference between opinion and fact is crucial; individuals should differentiate between subjective viewpoints and objective truths. Additionally, being aware of cognitive biases, such as confirmation bias, can help individuals recognize when they may favor information that aligns with their preexisting beliefs.

Engaging in discussions with others—especially those with differing viewpoints—can challenge assumptions and clarify misunderstandings. Lastly, developing media literacy skills allows individuals to navigate digital information critically, recognize reliable news outlets, and avoid misinformation.

Truthfulness is equally vital for self-reflection and personal development. Consider someone struggling with a fear of failure. If honest about their shortcomings, they can take actionable steps to overcome them, fostering resilience and improvement. This emphasis on personal growth can encourage and give hope to the audience. However, self-deception—blaming external factors or denying the issue—leaves them stagnant, unable to grow or move forward.

Truth as a Guiding Principle

Education is crucial in several ways to foster a commitment to truthfulness among individuals. It cultivates critical thinking skills, enabling students to analyze information, evaluate sources, and discern between fact and opinion. Education encourages inquiry and skepticism and helps individuals become more vigilant information consumers incorporating ethics and integrity into curricula to instill the value of truthfulness from an early age. Discussions about the importance of honesty in personal and professional settings can shape moral reasoning and character development.

Education promotes open dialogue and diverse perspectives, allowing students to engage in discussions that challenge their viewpoints. This exposure teaches the necessity of understanding others' truths while reinforcing the importance of being truthful themselves.

Creating an environment that prioritizes honesty—such as encouraging teachers and students to model truthful behavior—can strengthen a culture of integrity within educational institutions.

Educating individuals about the consequences of misinformation and the social responsibilities tied to truth helps them recognize the impact of their actions on the community, fostering a more significant commitment to truthfulness. Ultimately, truth is the bedrock upon which progress, trust, justice, and self-improvement are built. It provides a stable foundation for navigating life's complexities, ensuring individuals and societies act responsibly and ethically. Untruth prevents meaningful advancement and ethical decision-making.

In distinguishing truth from untruth, we uphold the principles that allow individuals and communities to thrive. Truth provides direction and purpose, enabling us to face challenges with integrity and clarity, while untruth undermines the very fabric of understanding and progress.

References

American Psychological Association. (n.d.). The psychology of truth and lies: Impacts on decision-making and trust. Retrieved from https://www.apa.org

Bok, S. (1999). Lying: Moral choice in public and private life. New York, NY: Vintage Books.

DePaulo, B. M., Kashy, D. A., Kirkendol, S. E., Wyer, M. M., & Epstein, J. A. (1996). Lying in everyday life. Journal of Personality and Social Psychology, 70(5), 979–995. https://doi.org/10.1037/0022-3514.70.5.979

FactCheck.org. (n.d.). Fighting misinformation: Tools and techniques for discerning truth. Retrieved from https://www.factcheck.org

Lewandowsky, S., Ecker, U. K., & Cook, J. (2017). Beyond misinformation: Understanding and coping with the "post-truth" era. Journal of Applied Research in Memory and Cognition, 6(4), 353–369. https://doi.org/10.1016/j.jarmac.2017.07.008

PolitiFact. (n.d.). Strategies to identify truth in a post-truth era. Retrieved from https://www.politifact.com

Rosenthal, R. (2002). The honesty gap: Social lying and its consequences. Cambridge, MA: Harvard University Press.

Snopes. (n.d.). Discerning truth from untruth: A practical guide. Retrieved from https://www.snopes.com

Trevino, L. K., & Nelson, K. A. (2016). Managing business ethics: Straight talk about how to do it right (7th ed.). Hoboken, NJ: Wiley.

Wardle, C., & Derakhshan, H. (2017). Information disorder: Toward an interdisciplinary framework for research and policymaking. Council of Europe. Retrieved from https://www.coe.int

Zimbardo, P., & Boyd, J. (2008). The time paradox: The new psychology of time that will change your life. New York, NY: Free Press.

www.ingramcontent.com/pod-product-compliance
Lightning Source LLC
Chambersburg PA
CBHW041933260326
41914CB00010B/1283